PHILIP FIRSOV

ART

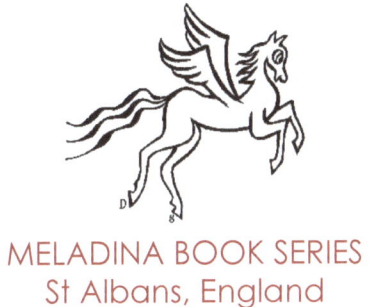

MELADINA BOOK SERIES
St Albans, England

Philip Firsov ART

CONTENTS

INTRODUCTION	4
BIOGRAPHY	6
PAINTINGS	9
MURALS	39
WATERCOLOURS	43
DRAWINGS	47
ETCHINGS	52
SCULPTURES	59

Cover photos © by Dasha & Mari

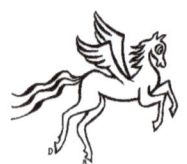

MELADINA BOOK SERIES
St Albans, England

Copyright © 2018 Philip Firsov, pictures and text
The book designed by © Dmitri N. Smirnov
All rights reserved
ISBN-13: 978-1984291868
ISBN-10: 1984291866
Printed: CreateSpace
For Amazon
Charleston
USA

PICTURES

PAINTINGS • MURALS • WATERCOLOURS • DRAWINGS • ETCHINGS

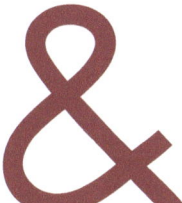

SCULPTURES

I make paintings, sculptures and films most of which end up looking like scattered fragments of a lost theatrical machine. They are based on musical instruments and characters I met on my many travels around Eastern Europe and the Mediterranean.

Having been born in the West of Moscow with my earliest memories being the contrast between the monotonous courtyards of Soviet blocks and one of the noblest Naryshkin Baroque churches, The Lykov Trinity, my eyes were drawn to the eclecticism of the Baroque and Oriental architecture and its harmony with nature. Later as my family moved to the UK, I was sketching the gothic architecture of Cambridge and enjoying the beauty of the Renaissance in the National Gallery. I began painting and drawing musicians in the rehearsal's of my family's musical projects, travelling with them around European music festivals and appreciating the art collections. I was taught by a private tutor who was trained at the Repin Academy and studied painting in 3 Universities in London, before specializing also in sculptural carving at City and Guilds, studying traditional and historic techniques. I was involved in several European art residencies and exhibitions in Romania, Italy and Germany. Inspired by classicism, I present the co-existence of ancient and modern worlds in paintings, often taking reference from my own travels, dealing with the burden of history and the emigration of peoples and their identities. It was through having to explain my origin to others that I had to reinvent the worlds of Russian and European heritage.

Philip Firsov

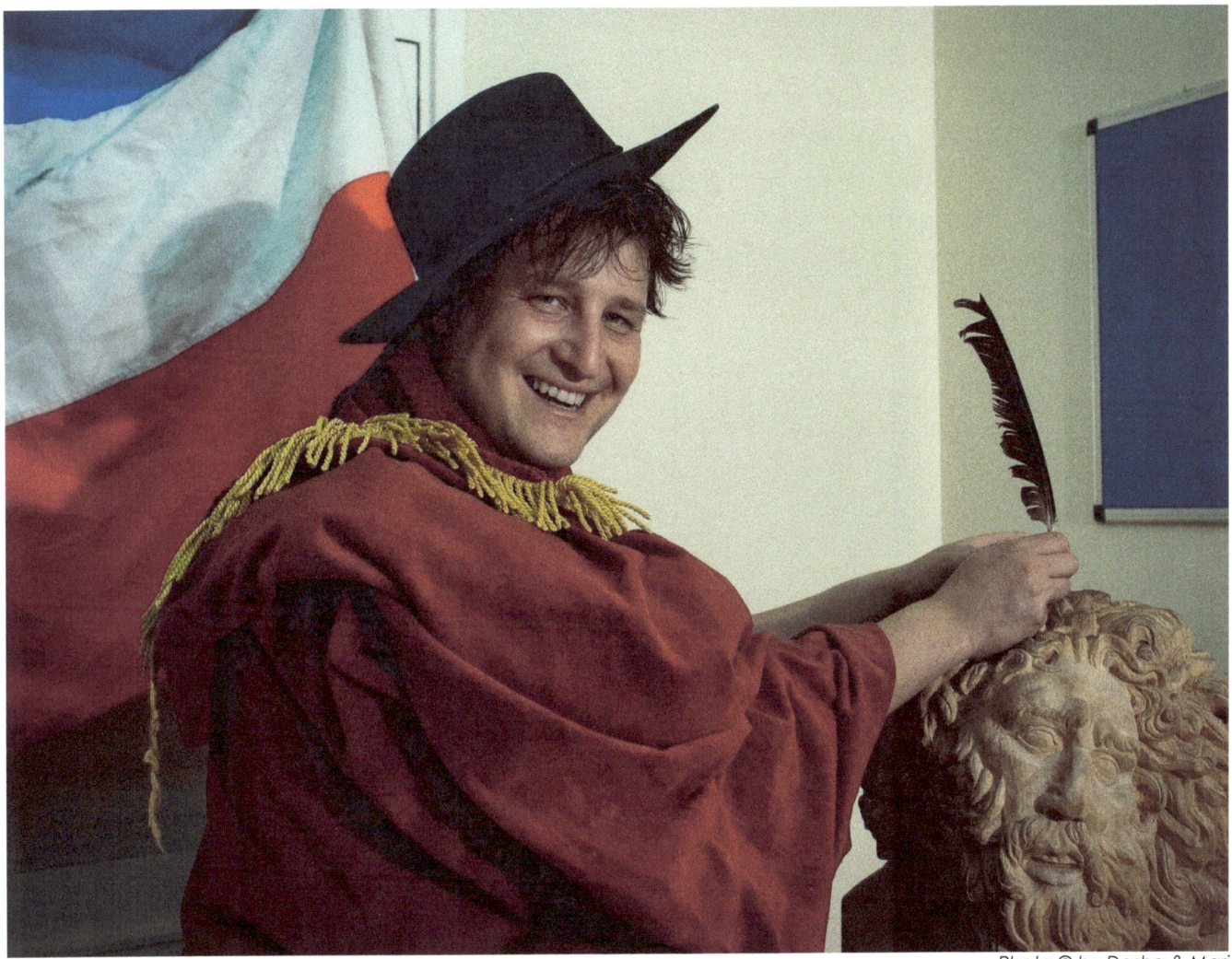

Philip Firsov and his Laocoon Bust

Photo © by Dasha & Mari

Philip Firsov (born 8 April 1985 in Moscow) is a British painter and sculptor of Russian origin. Born in the family of two Russian composers Elena Firsova and Dmitri Smirnov, he left Russia in the age of 6. The family settled in England. From the age of 15 he studied art privately with Russian artist and restorer Alexander Kolesnik, and then continued his education in Central Saint Martins College of Art and Design, Foundation, Slade School of Fine Art, BA in Fine Art, and Prince's Drawing School, Post Graduate Scheme.

Education

2014–2016: Studied Historic and Ornamental Woodcarving, Diploma at City and Guilds School of Art in Kennington Park Rd. London
2008–2009: Prince's Drawing School, Post Graduate Scheme
2007: Artist in Residence, Cucuteni Symposium "Human", Iasi, Romania; Diploma of Excellence
2007: Painting Symposium, Campina, Romania; Diploma of Excellence
2004–2008: Slade School of Fine Art, BA in Fine Art
2003–2004: Central Saint Martin's, Foundation
2000–2005: Privately studied Atelier of Russian Artist and Restorer, Alexander Kolesnik, Acme Studios, Deptford

Solo exhibitions

2017: 1 July. Dante Divine Comedy etchings. Official artist. Russian Summer Ball, The Honorable Artillery Company, City Road, London
2017: 1 July. Dante Divine Comedy etchings. Russian Jubilee Ball, Foyer, Draper's Hall, London
2016: December. Solo Exhibition No. 1 Primrose Street, London
2016: July. Official artist. Russian Summer Ball, Lancaster House, London
2015: November. Divine Comedy Triptych, ink drawing at Teatro della Tosse, Piazza Renato Negri, 6, Genova GE, Italy
2015: August. Divine Comedy Triptych, ink drawing at Chiesa di San Rocco, Corso IV Novembre, Asiago, Italy
2015: July. Official artist. Russian Summer Ball, Lancaster House, London
2014: July. Official artist. Russian Summer Ball, Cavalry and Guards Club, London
2013: 26 November – 1 December. "Entwined" The Crypt Gallery St Pancras New Church, Euston Rd NW1 London
2013: September. Nati Gallery, 22 Warren Street, London
2012: October Solo Exhibition, Nati Gallery, Warren Street London W1T 5LU
2012: Februaery Philip Firsov and Phoebe Cope. TwentyTwo to TwentySix. London
2011: 9–18 May "My Russia ReDrawn" — Solo Exhibition at Frameless Gallery, 20 Clerkenwell Green, London EC1
2010: October/November "Exodus" — Solo Exhibition at Frameless Gallery, 20 Clerkenwell Green, London EC1
2010: October Solo Exhibition in Supperclub Aclam Rd Portobello
2007: Exhibition of Cupola Gallery, Iasi, Romania
2007: Exhibition of sculptures and films, Brunel Museum, Rotherhithe, London
2006: Artist in Residence, Dartington Summer Music Festival (Devon), Shipon Gallery

2006: Artist in Residence, Oxford Contemporary Music Festival, Jacqueline du Pré music Building, St. Hilda's College, Oxford
2005: Cheltenham Triptych of Paintings, The Pitville Pump Room, Cheltenham Music Festival, Cheltenham
2005: Sculpture Installation, Window Gallery Central Saint Martin's, Charing Cross Road, London

Selected group exhibitions

2017: June. Etchings. Hampstead Art Fair, London
2016: April. Oxford and Cambridge Club, Pall Mall, London
2015: September. Parergon Gallery, Shepherd's Market, London
2011: November. Hanover Music Society. Exhibition of 3 paintings on Kubla Khan. Projection of works on Music Stage during the concert.
2011: October, Group Show Assisi Galleria Comunale. Contemporary Art Residency Ginestrelle. Sculpture of St Francis (in wood).
2010: June–August, Summer Contemporary, Fulham Art Fair by Salon Art Bizarre in association with Unique Art Gallery on 595 King's Road.
2010: 7–21 June, Art Exhibition '20 years of Russians in Britain', Europa Gallery, Sutton Library, St.Nicholas Way, Sutton, Surrey SM1 1EA
2008: Dialects: Part 1, Pushkin House (Russian Cultural Centre), Bloomsbury Way
2008: Paintings in Association with Salon Russe, Brunel Museum, Rotherhithe, London
2008: Russian Winter Season, 54 Gallery, Mayfair, London
2008: Paintings, Sculptures and Films at MC Motors, Dalston
2007: Film screenings Melange Social Club, Hackney, London

PAINTINGS

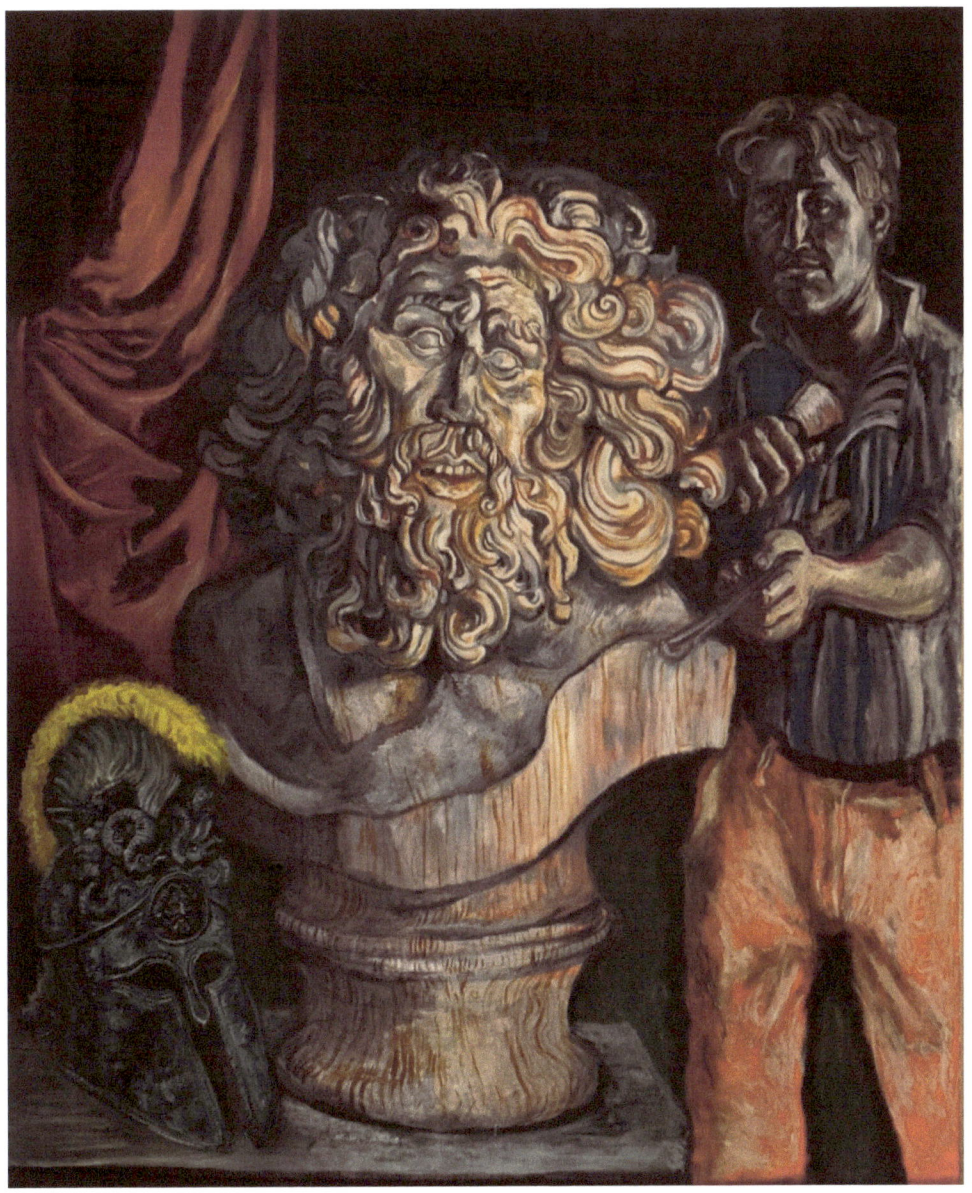

Self Portrait with Trojan Relics. Oil on canvas, 120 x 100 cm, 2017

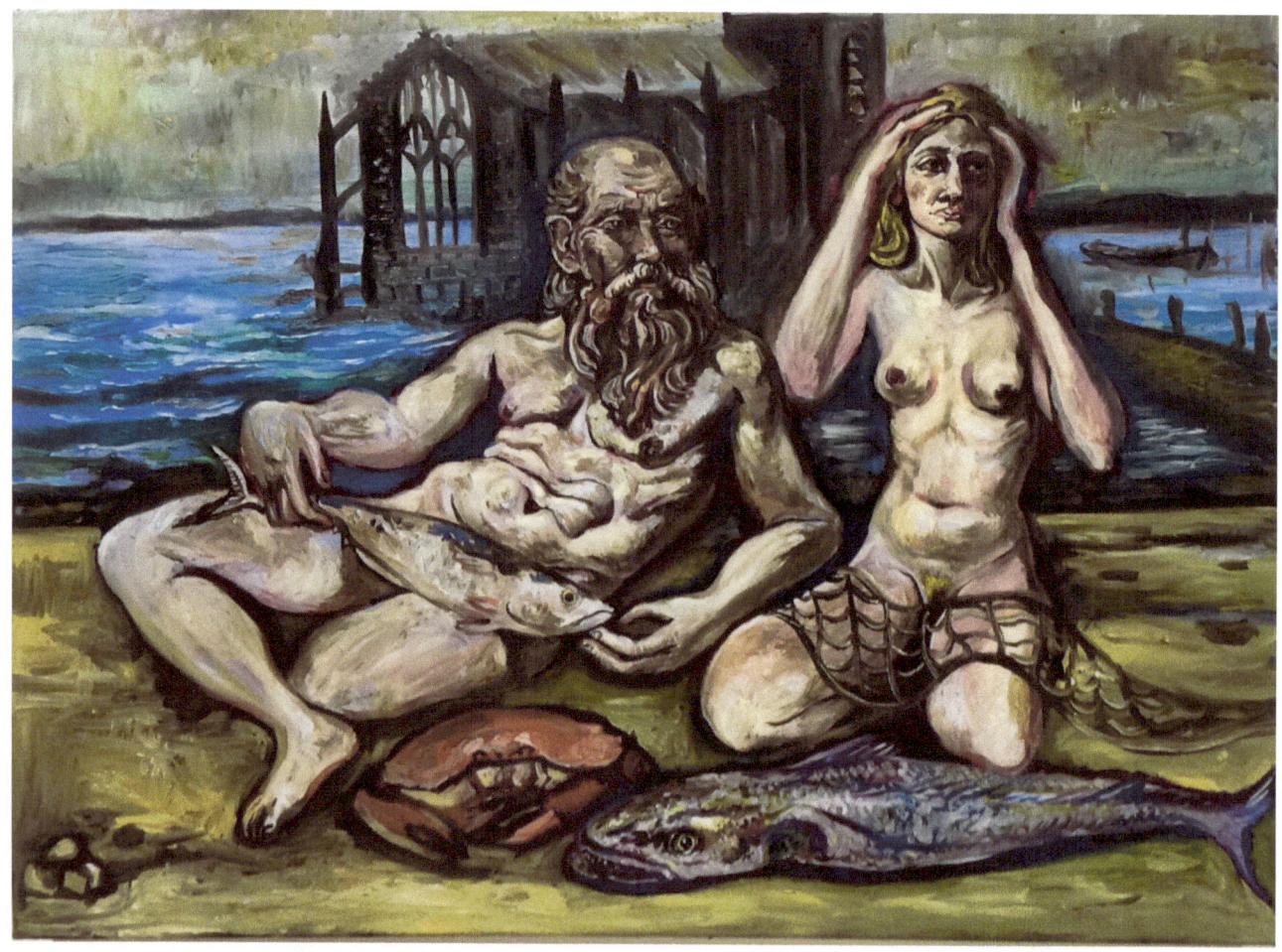

The Norfolk Fisherman's Catch. Oil on canvas, 60 x 80cm, 2017

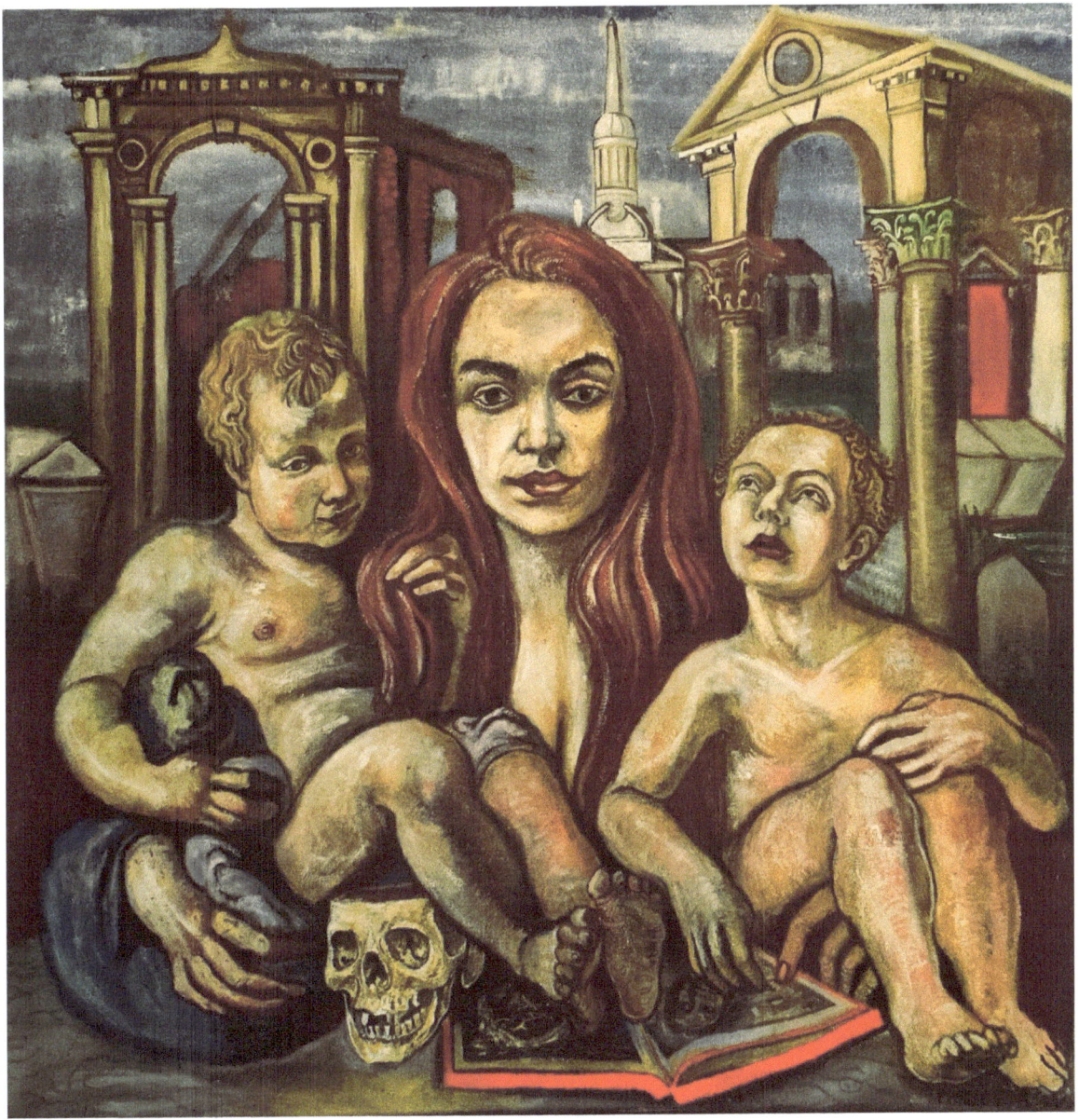

Madonna dei Gemelli. Oil on canvas, 100 x 100cm, 2017

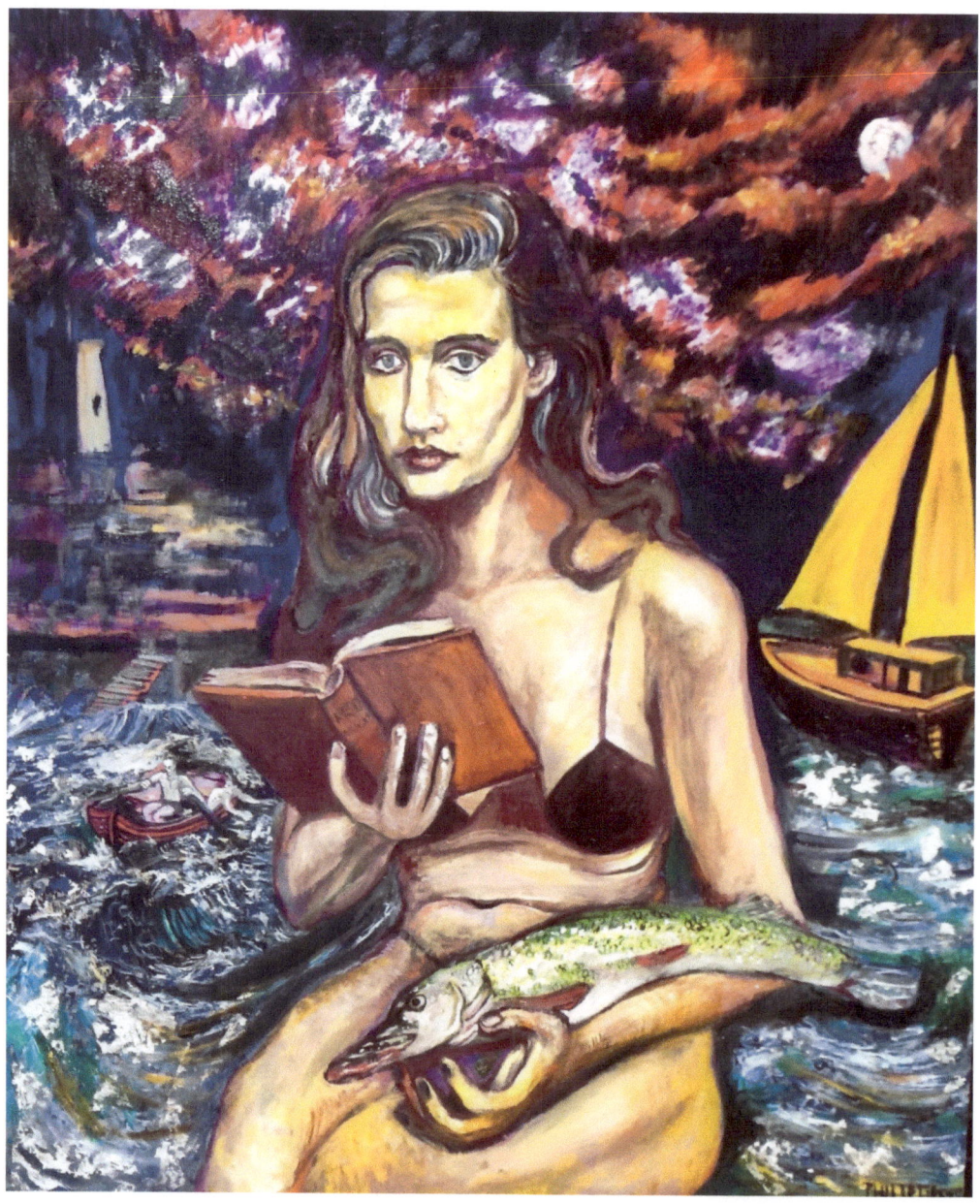

Madonna del Luccio. Oil on canvas, 100 x 80 cm, 2017

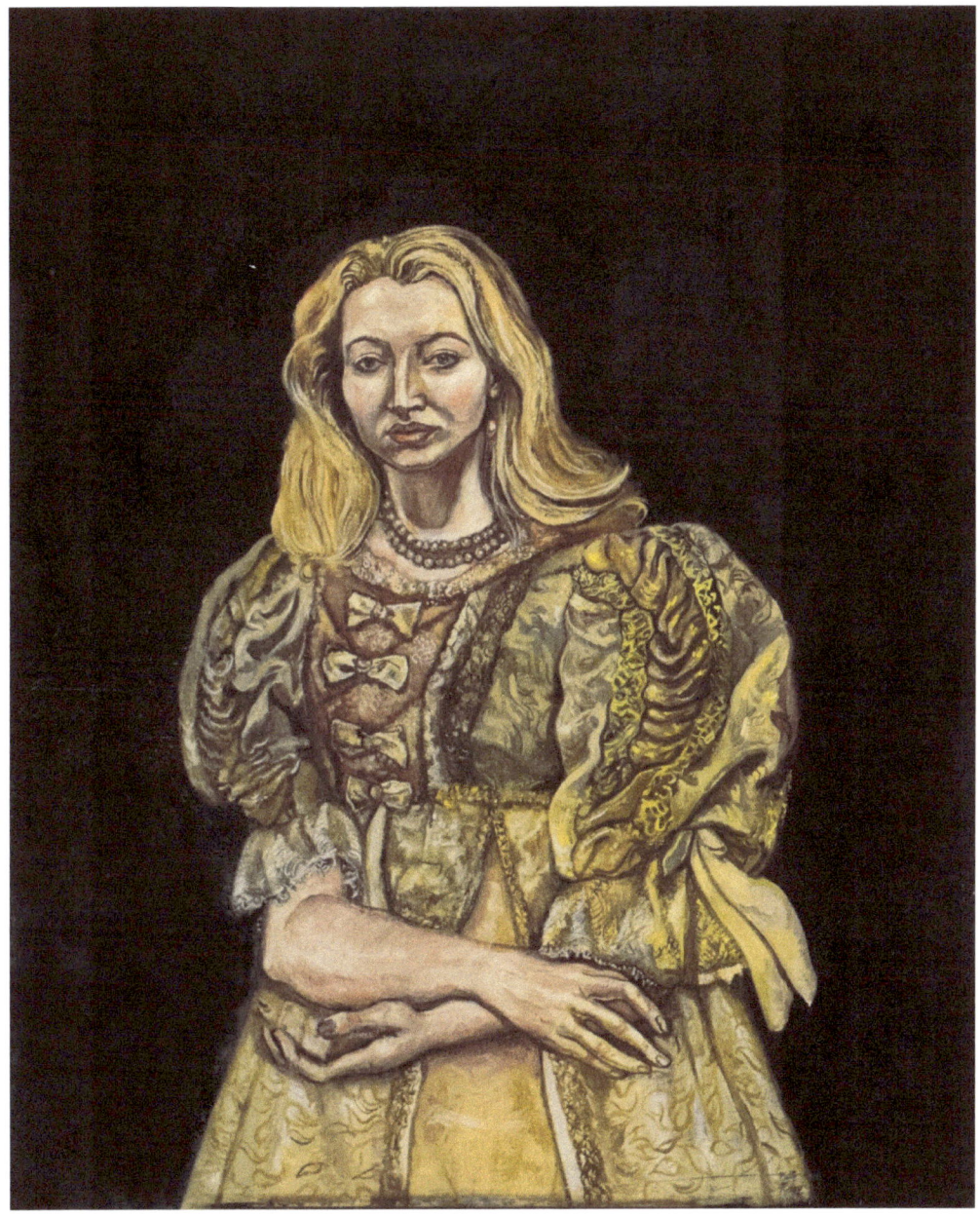

Portrait of Joanna in costume. Oil on canvas, 100 x 80 cm, 2016

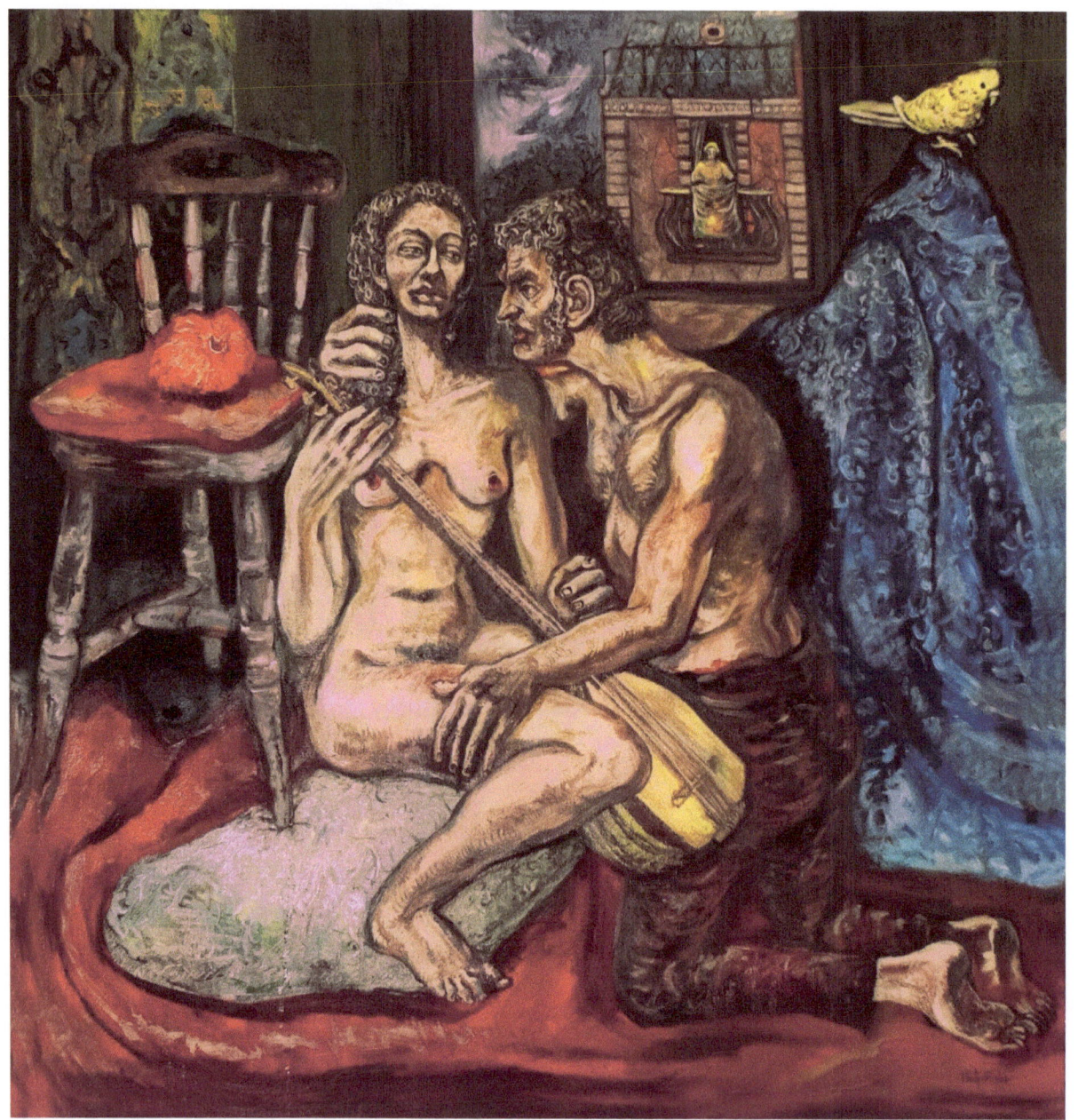

Pompeian Satyr in the Apartment. Oil on Canvas, 100 x 100cm, 2014

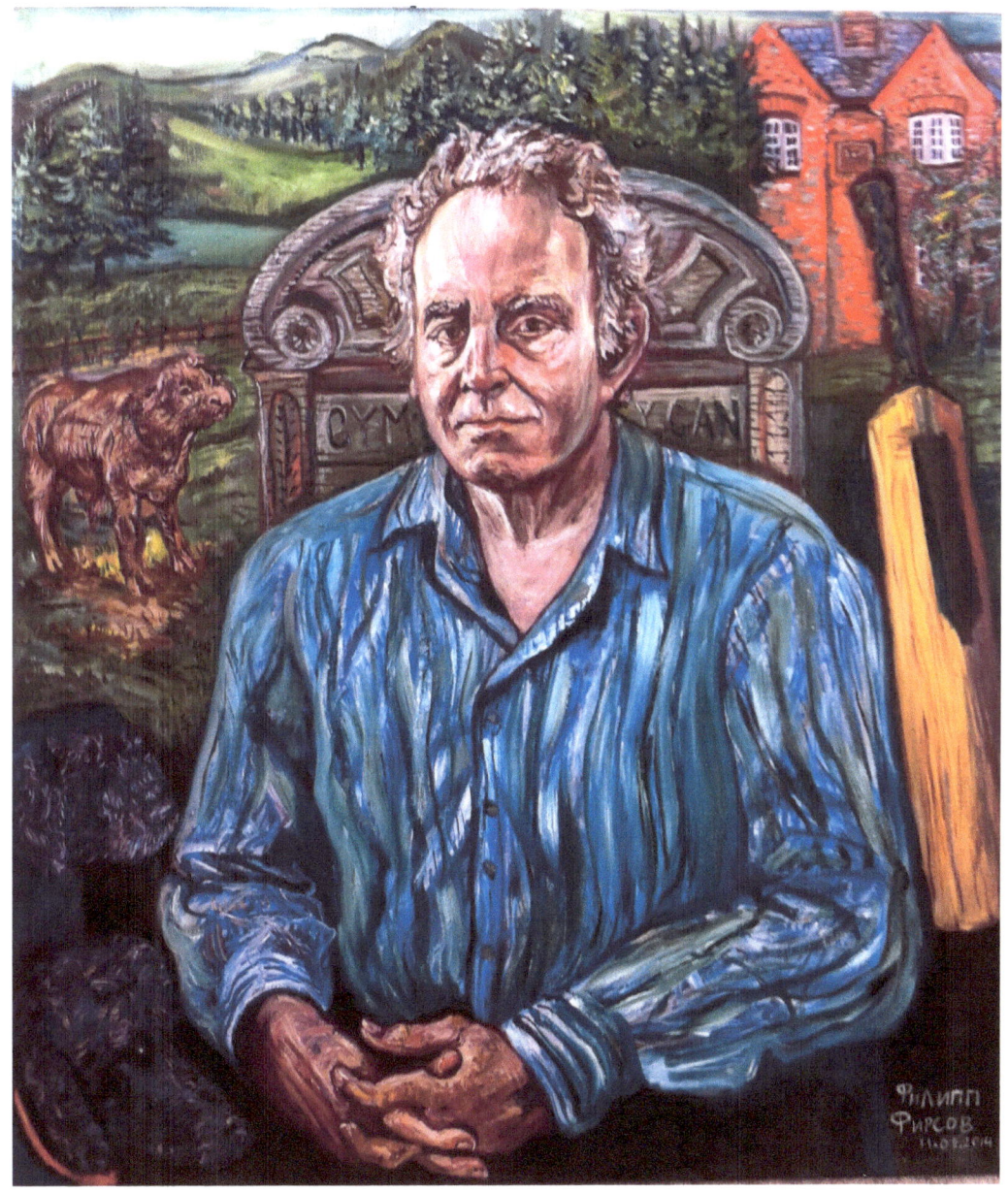

Peter Prior. Oil on canvas, 2014. Private collection

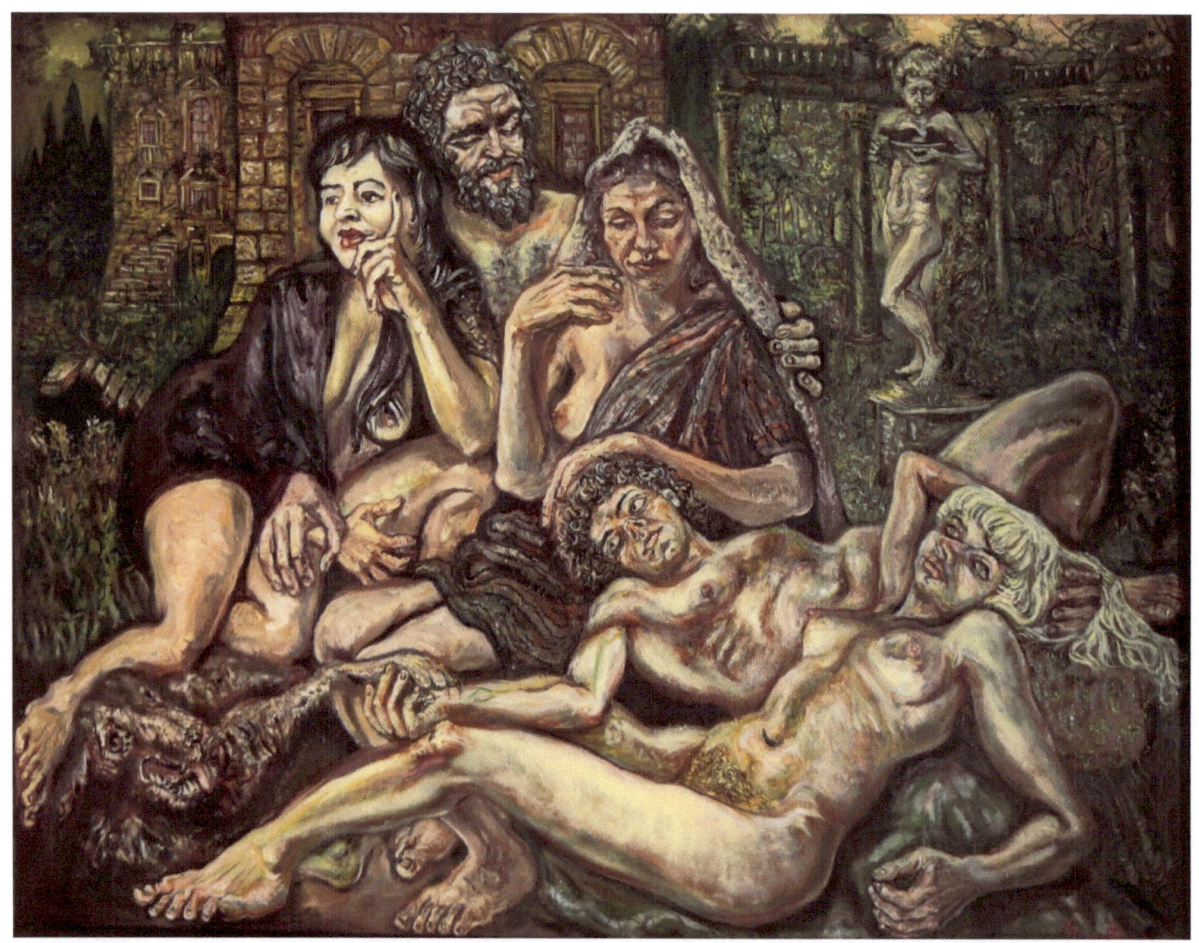

The Nude Picnic. Oil on

The Nude Picnic

A group of bored young people are exhausted after a night of partying in a garden of an abandoned Italian Villa. I found many empty villas in Italy that looked like beautiful palaces, but are often owned by large organisations like the Vatican, who have no interest in re-developing them, so they remain as ruins and zeitgeists. The villa here in the background hints at the royal residence at San Giorgio a Cremano in the *Amalfi* bay, this looks like it was left abandoned since a serious fire, even though it is also the home of the first train line in Italy, built for the King of Naples for his waterside residence removed from the centre.

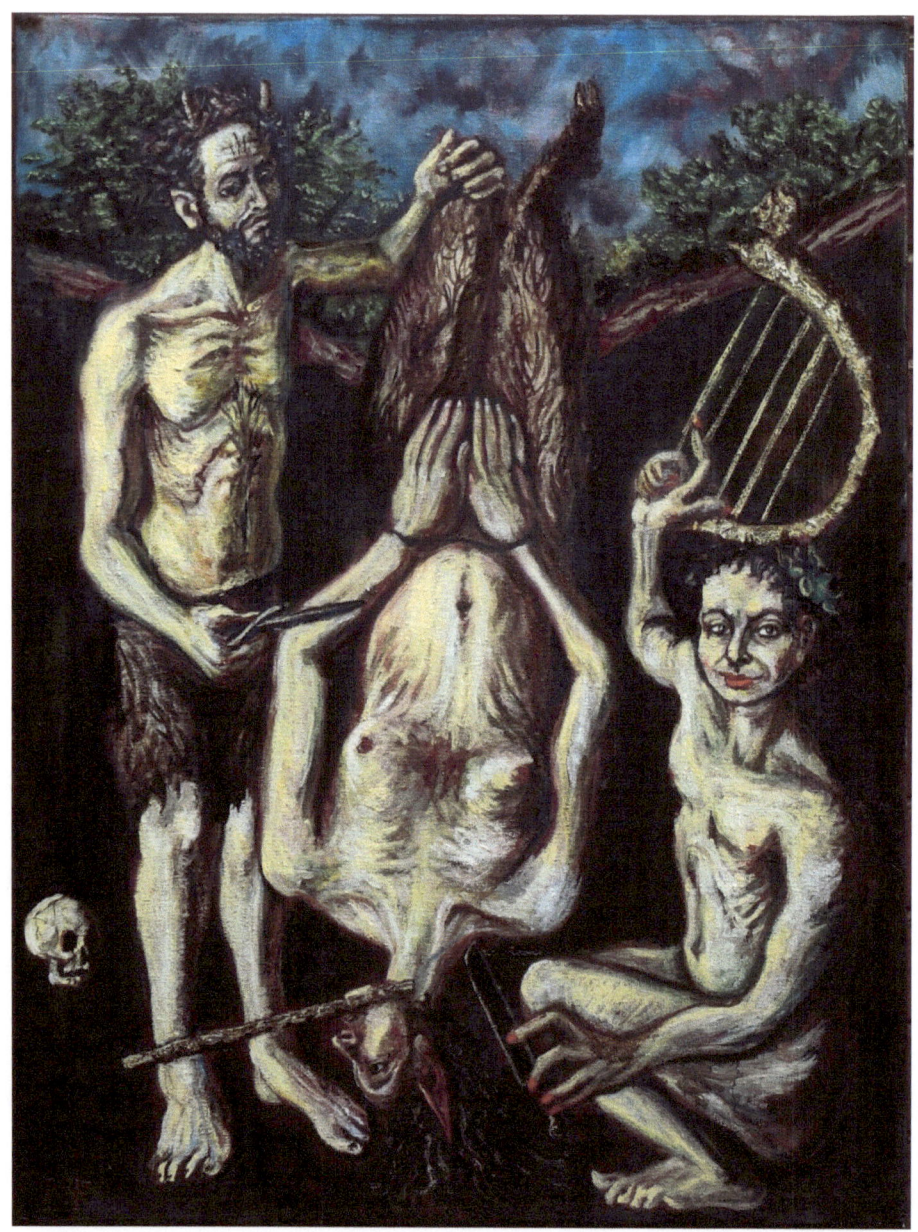

Marsyas and Apollo. Oil on canvas, 2013

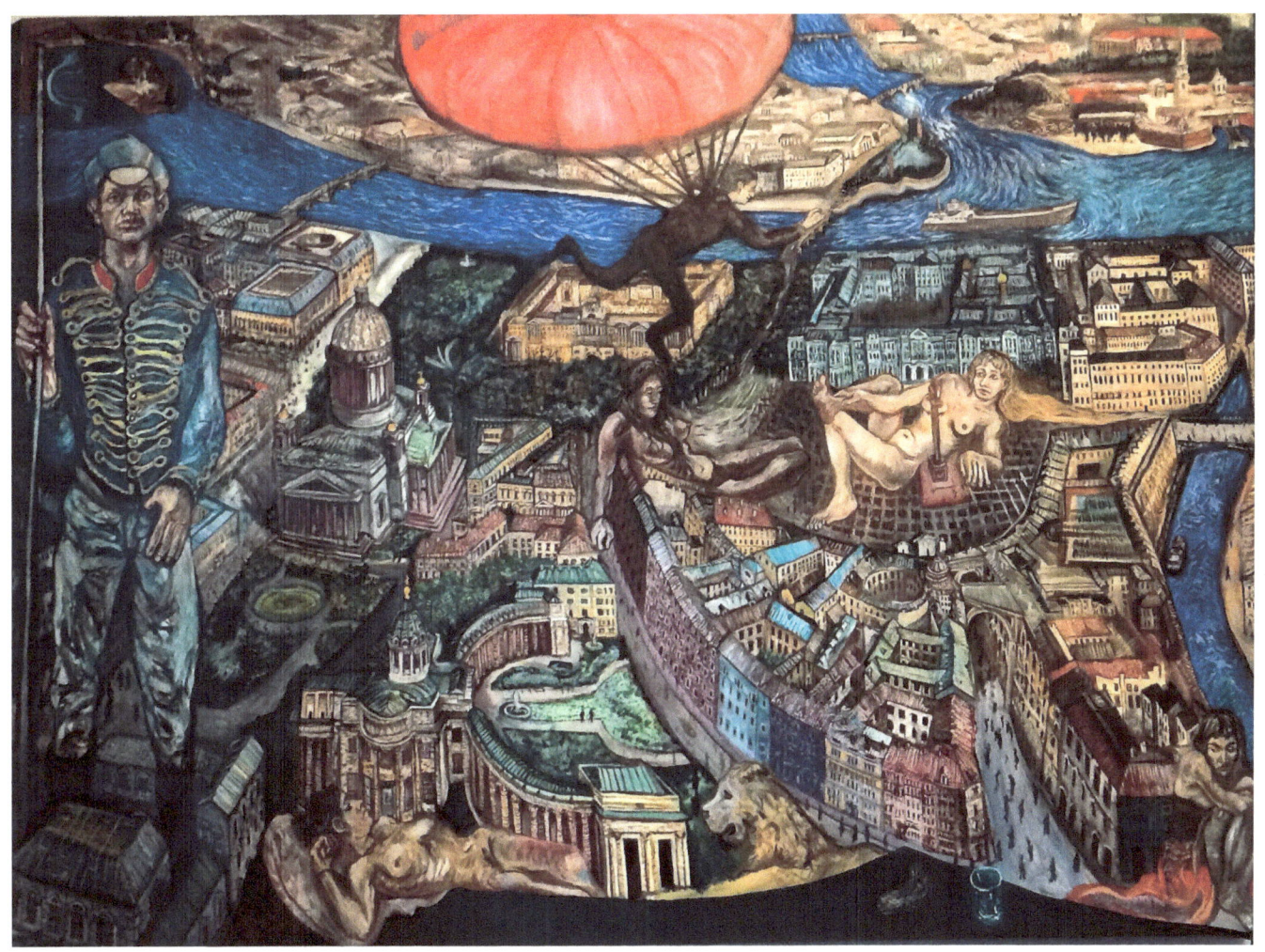

St Petersburg. Oil on canvas, 2013

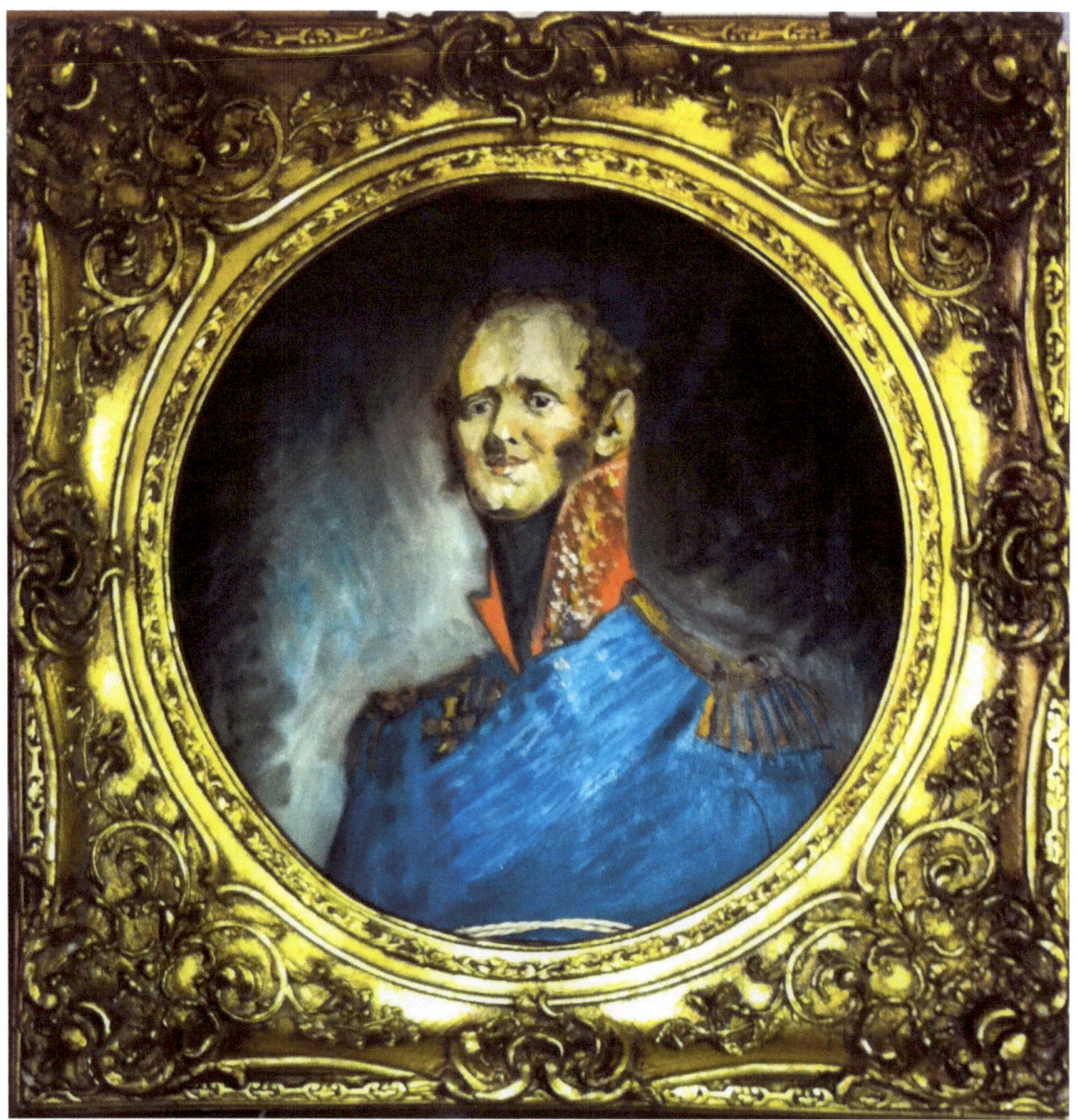

Alexander 1st. Oil on canvas, 2013

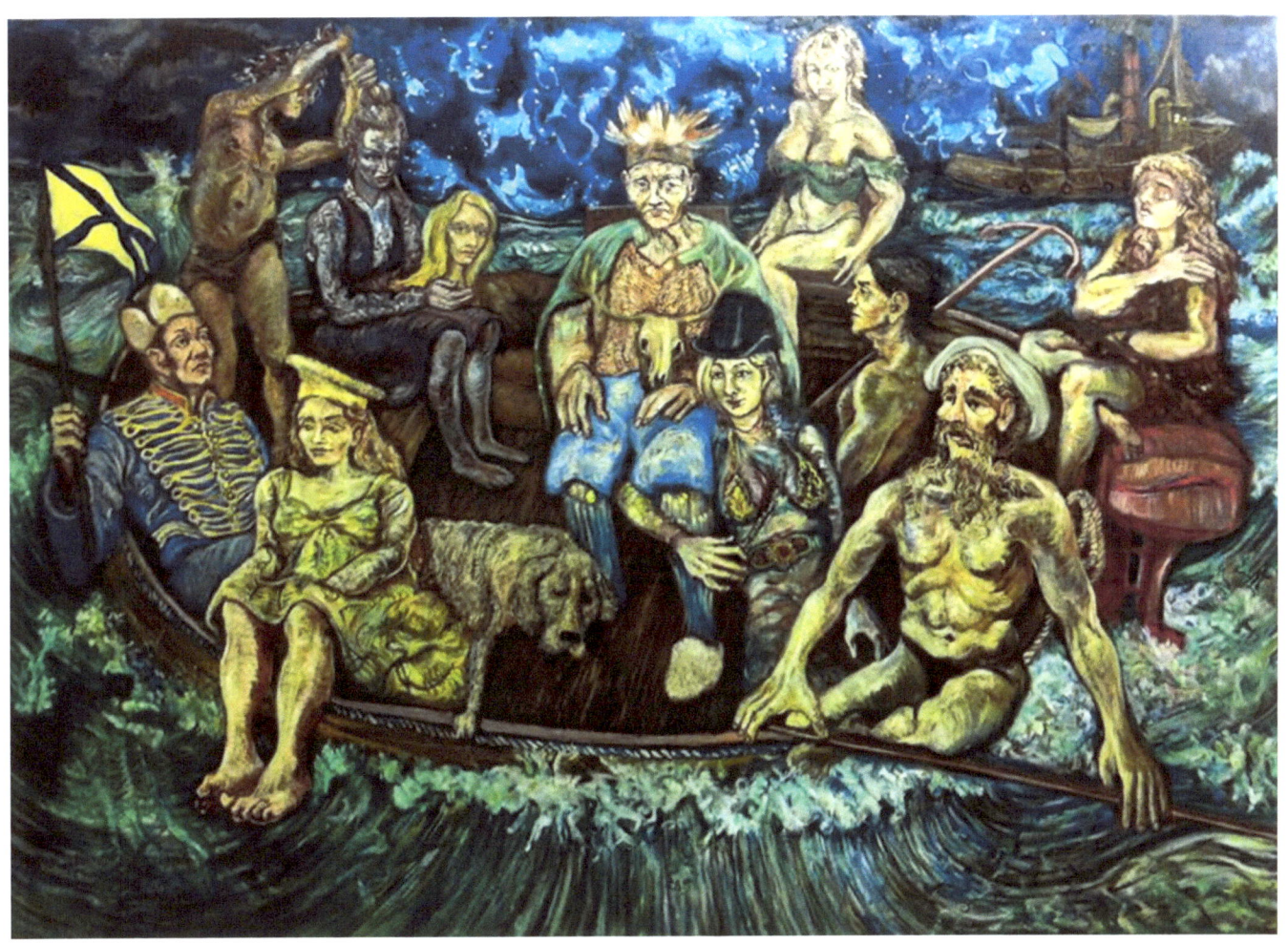

The Tempest. Oil on canvas, 200 x 140 cm, 2013

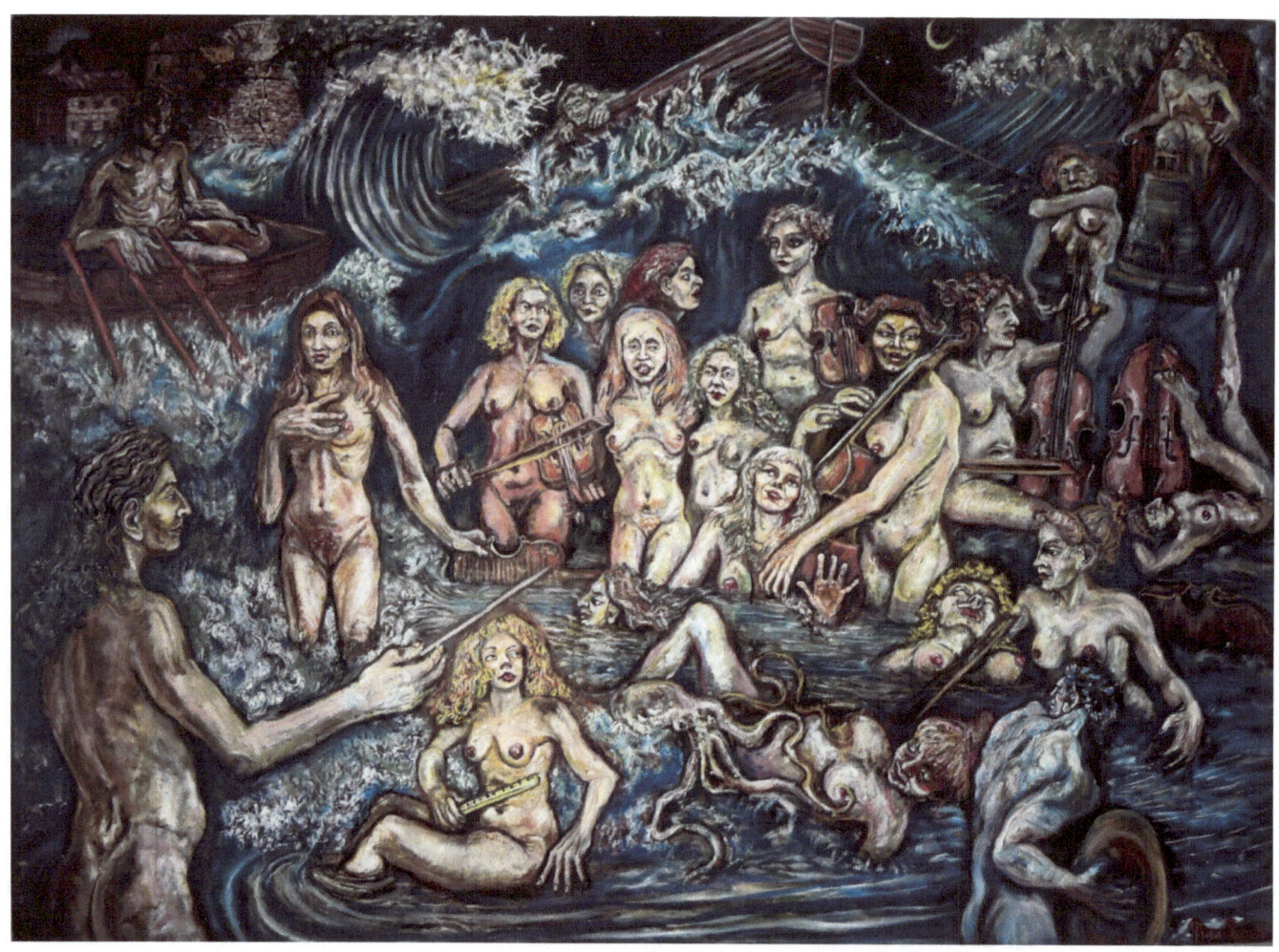

The Naked Orchestra. Oil on canvas, 200 x 140 cm, 2012

The Naked Orchestra

This picture comes from the concerts that my sister conducted recently. They were playing a difficult program including a beautiful piece by my mother Elena Firsova, which gave me the idea of a naked orchestra of sirens in a tempestuous Ocean. I had travelled in the summer around the Shakespearian settings in the Adriatic and saw places that looked like the "Illyria" described in Twelfth Night and The Tempest. In the background I painted from a watercolour sketch I made of the city of Corcula, the birthplace of Marco Polo. The boy on the boat represents narcissistic Marco Polo, who travels past the sirens, but is only interested in writing his book rather than in stopping and getting lured in by the nymphs.

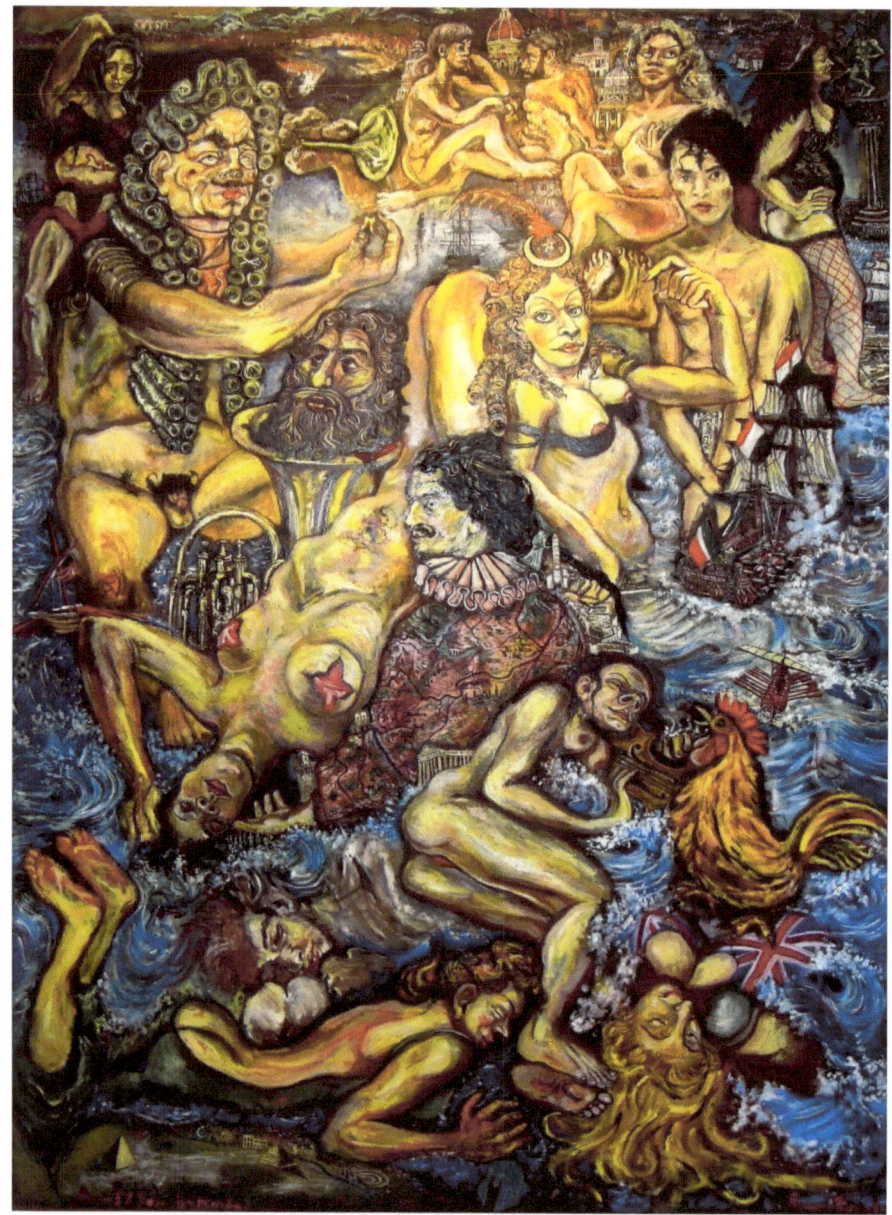

In the 39th Kingdom. Oil on canvas, 140 x 200 cm, 2011-12

In the 39th Kingdom

A serpentine composition of giants that transform themselves into sea nymphs and glaucuses among the geographical landmarks of the Italian Islands and Peninsula. In the centre is Sicily with a metamorphosed Etna, in the guise of a dwarfed bust of Peter the Great, whose reptilian head erupts out of a Piccadilly. On his red velvet Landsknecht jacket appears a map of Sicily with its temples of Agrigento, Enna, Piazza Armerina, Erice, Palermo, Syracuse and Catania, and a lion's silhouette at Corleone. This triangle is propped up by three party girls, who represent the three legs of Sicilian heraldry—they are the mythological sirens of Sicily. In between the figures and waves there are different scaled symbols of the identity of the kingdom of the Two Sicilies. The painting is entitled "*In the 39th Kingdom*" because of the coincidence of the Italian telephone prefix "+39" with the traditional beginning of many Russian fairytales "*V Tri-Devyatom Tsarstve*" (In the 39th Kingdom).

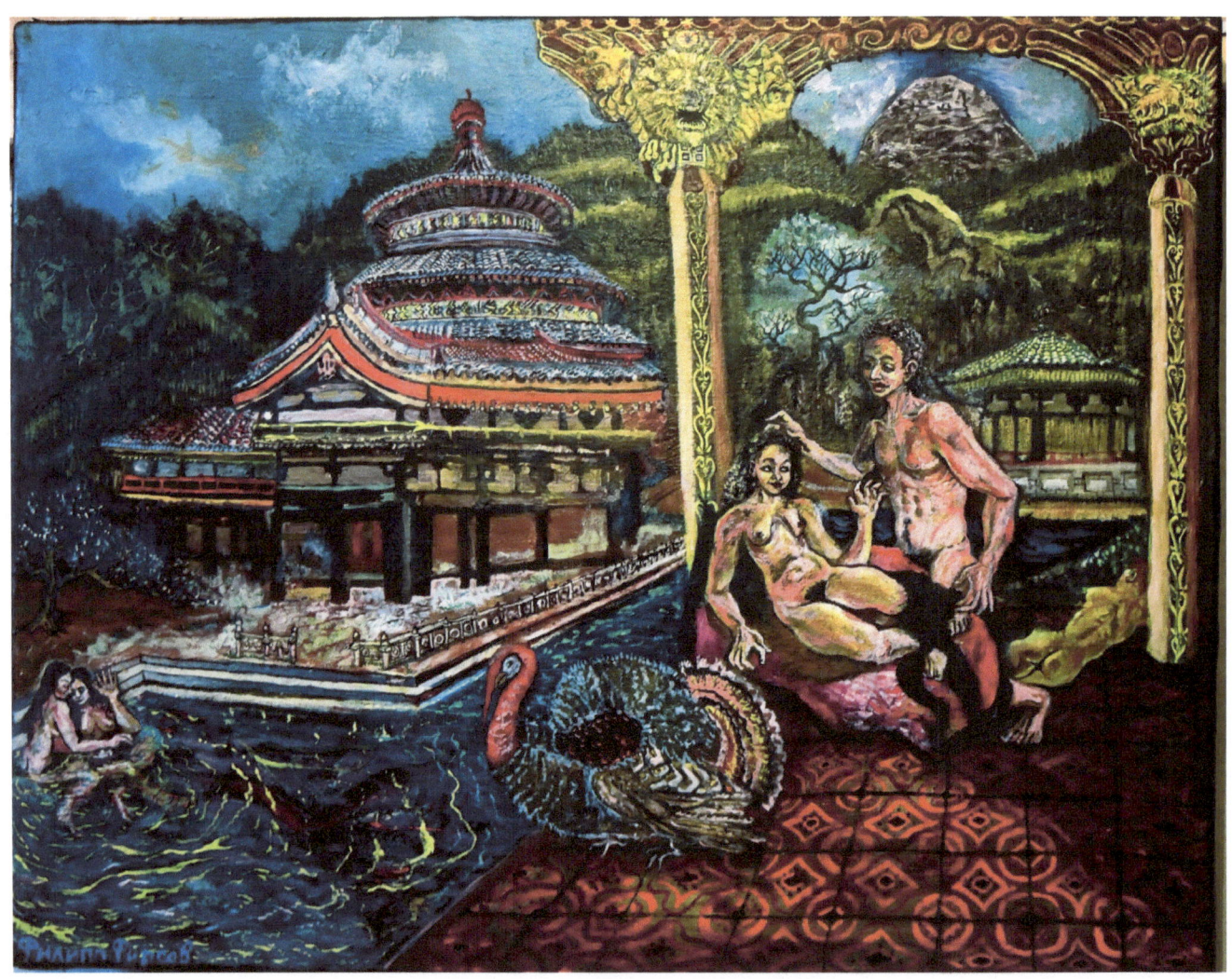

Kubla Khan: 1. The Pleasure Dome. Oil on canvas, 2011. Private collection

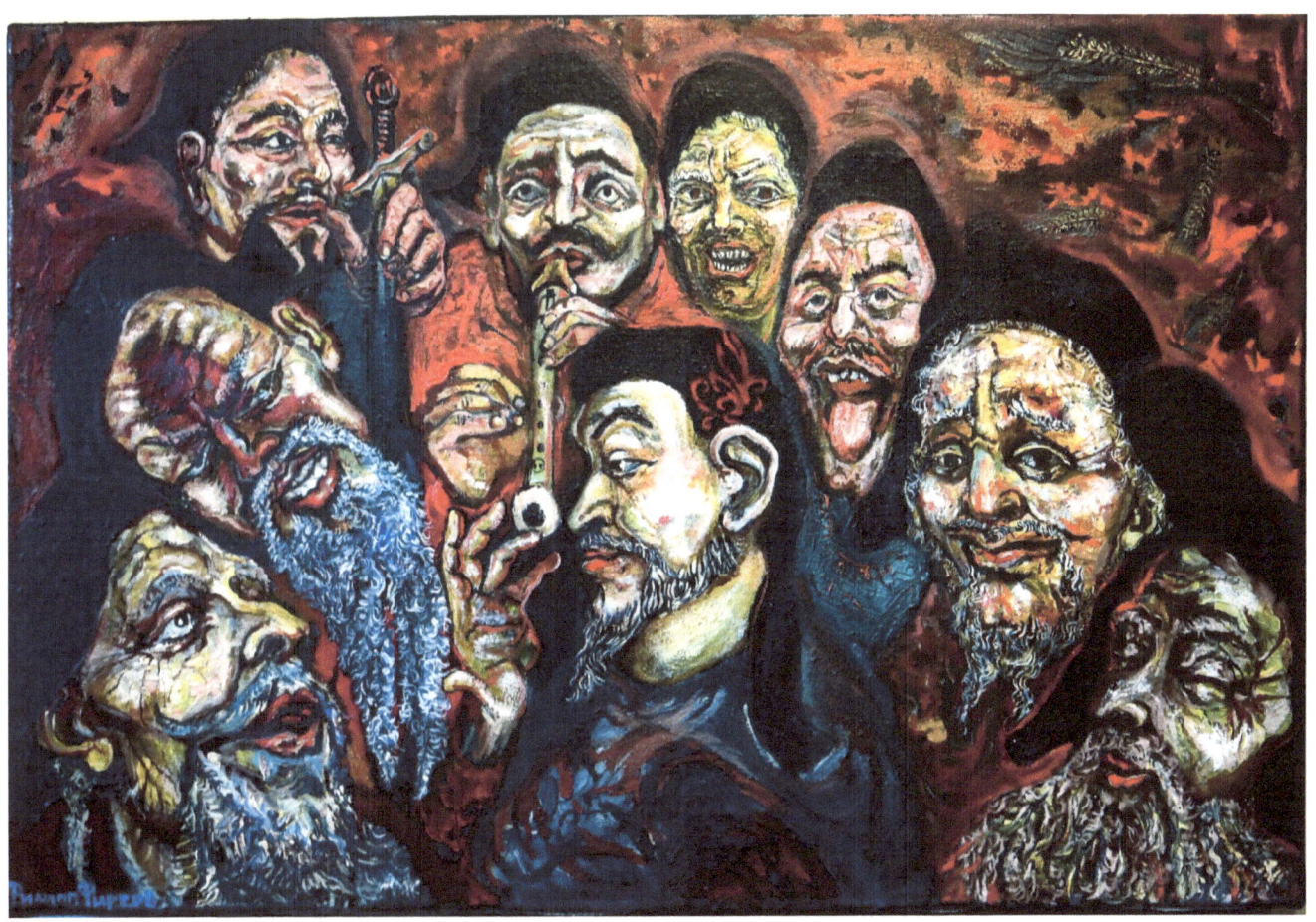

Kubla Khan: 2. The Ancestral Voices. Oil on canvas, 2011. Private collection

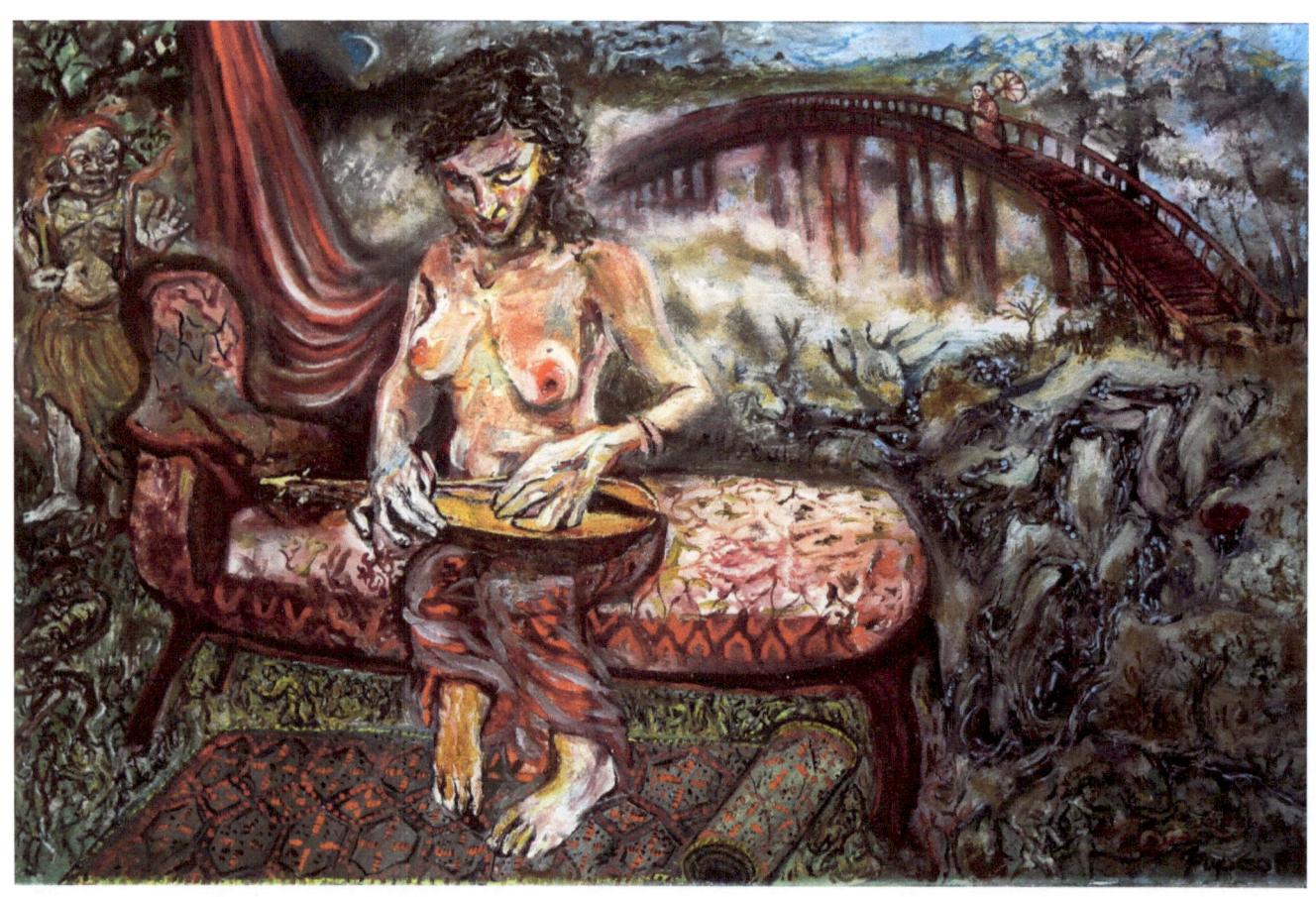

Kubla Khan: 3. A Damsel with a Dulcimer. Oil on canvas, 2011. Private collection

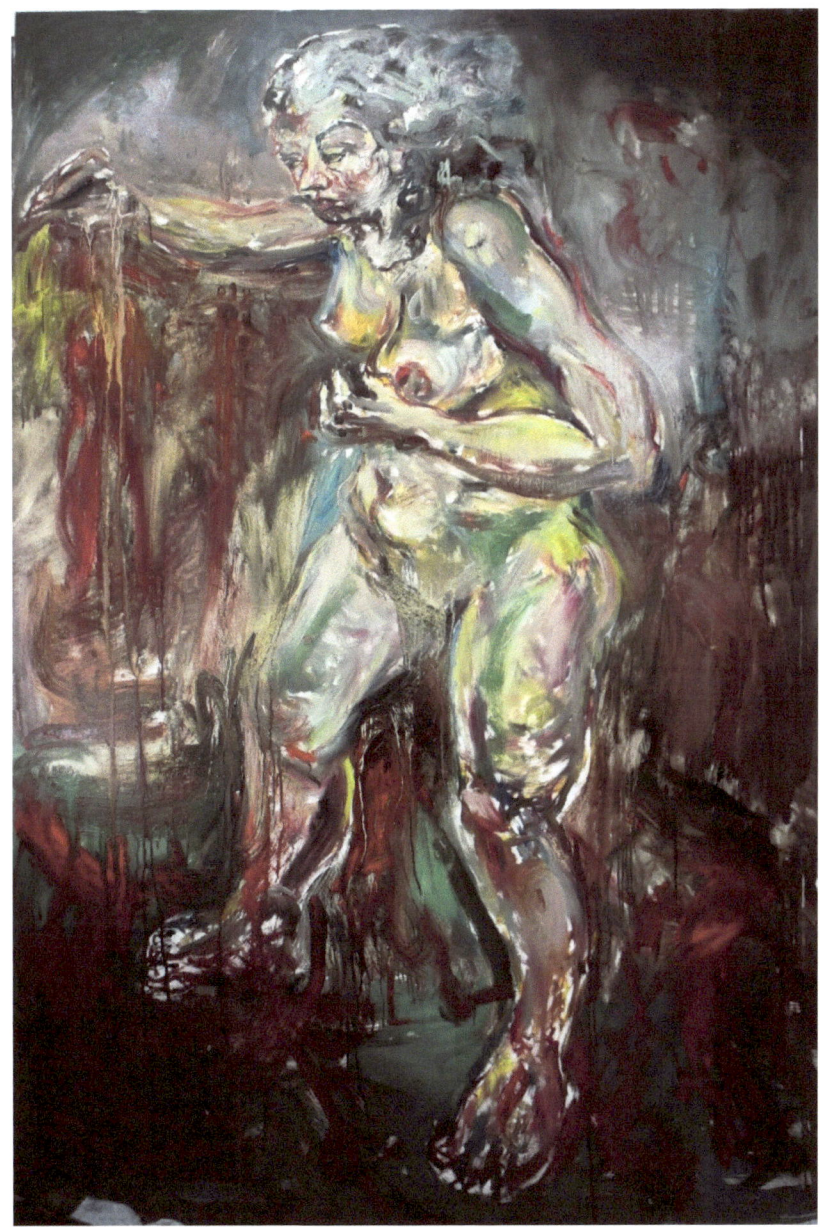

Woman. Oil on canvas, 140 x 200 cm, 2010. Private collection

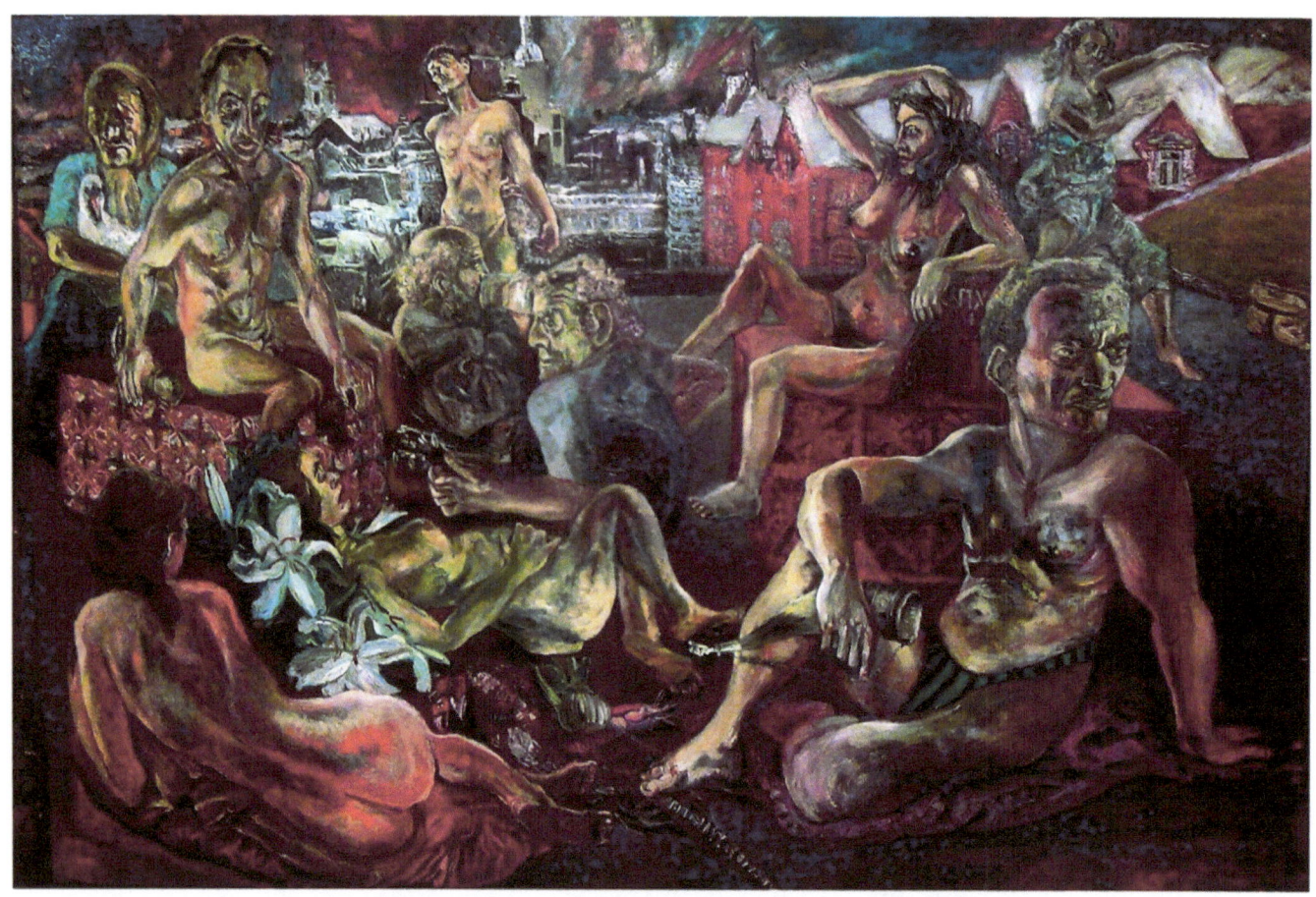

Ironic Roofs. Oil on canvas, 200 x 140 cm, 2009

Ironic Roofs

In *Ironic Roofs* I set sun-bathing life models and ageing, scantily dressed alcoholics on a snow covered roof. To emphasize how during snowfall in Britain, the whole country stops as if it's the end of civilisation. I am trying to evoke the atmosphere of anonymity and the indifference of people to each other in the city, by showing these compacted characters who gaze past each other and beyond the picture viewer. I strive to represent characters with a loving compassion—with humanistic empathy. The characters displaced away from their original context either group together or try to exclude each other and avoid mutual contact, but still prudently coexist in the crowd of immigrants and locals.

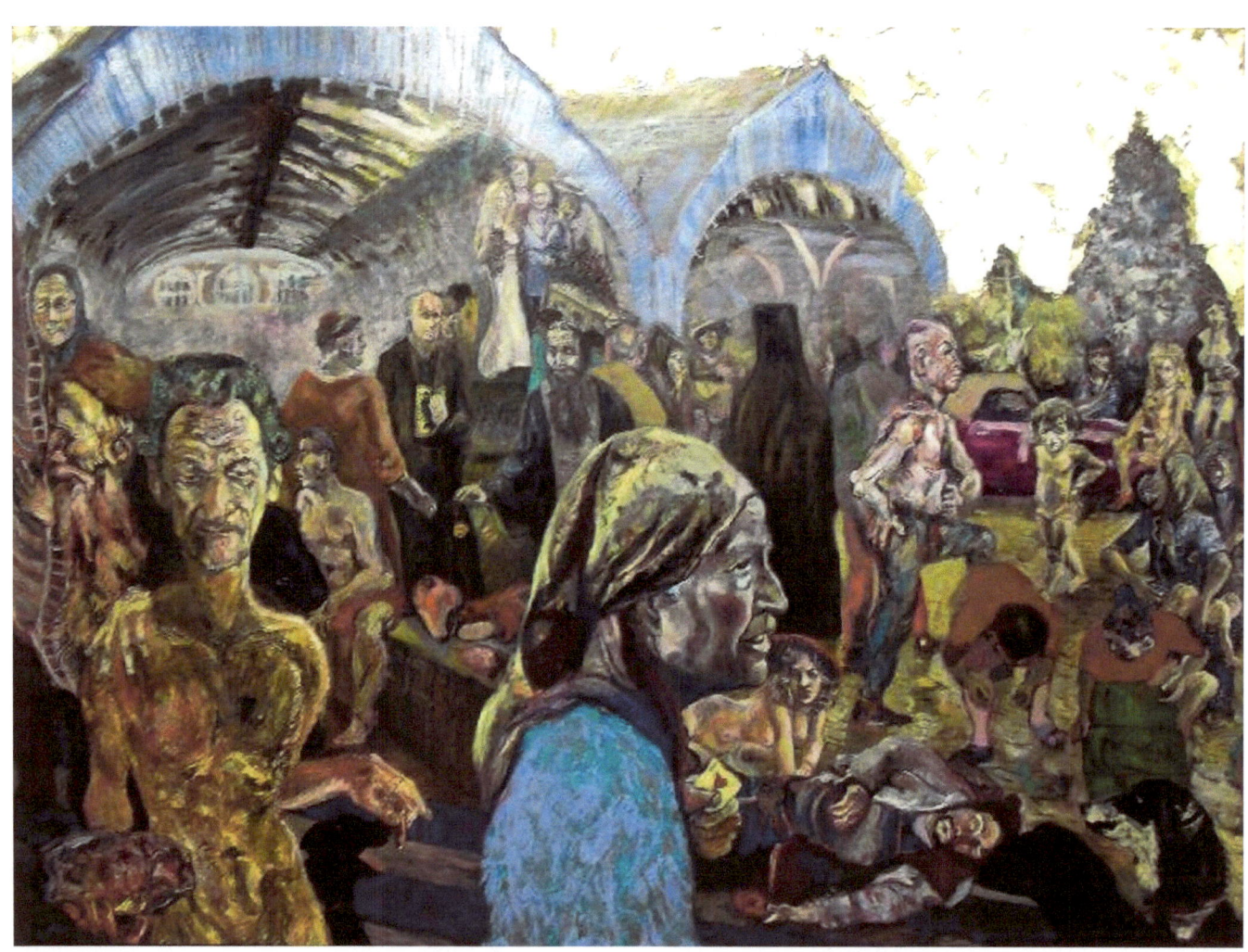

Vauxhall. Oil on canvas, 200 x 140 cm, 2009

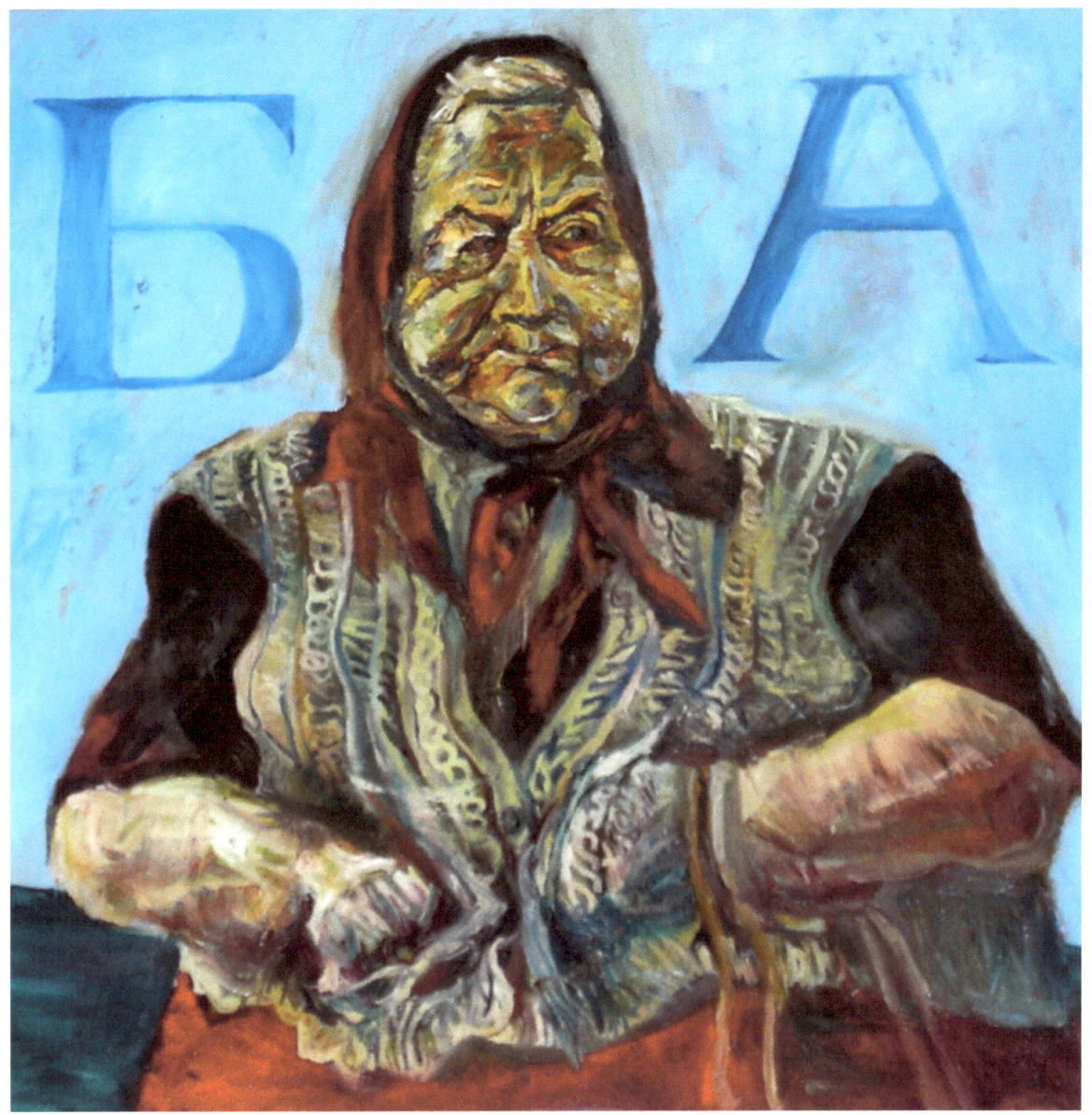

BA. Oil on canvas, 120 x 120, 2019

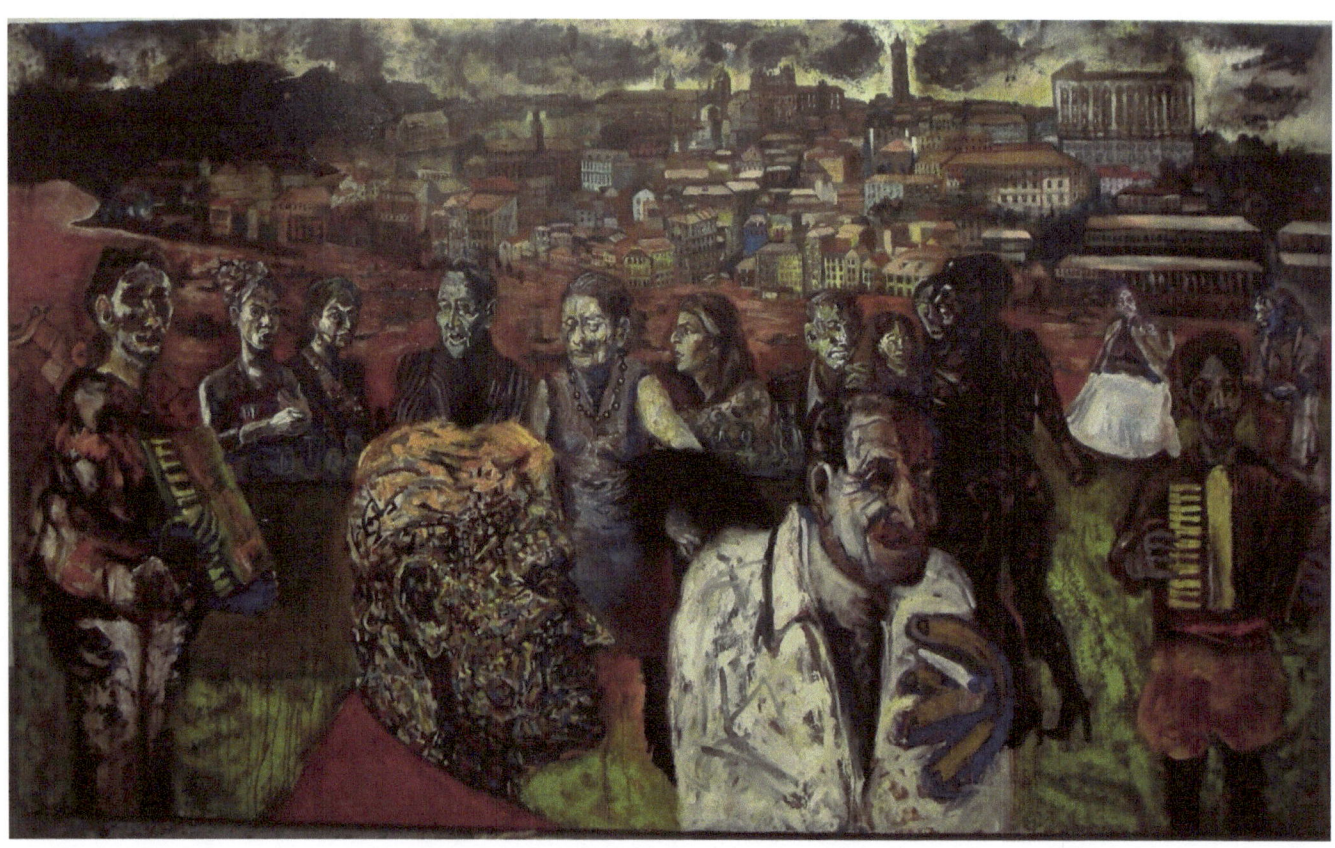

The Marriage. Oil on canvas, 300 x 180 cm, 2007

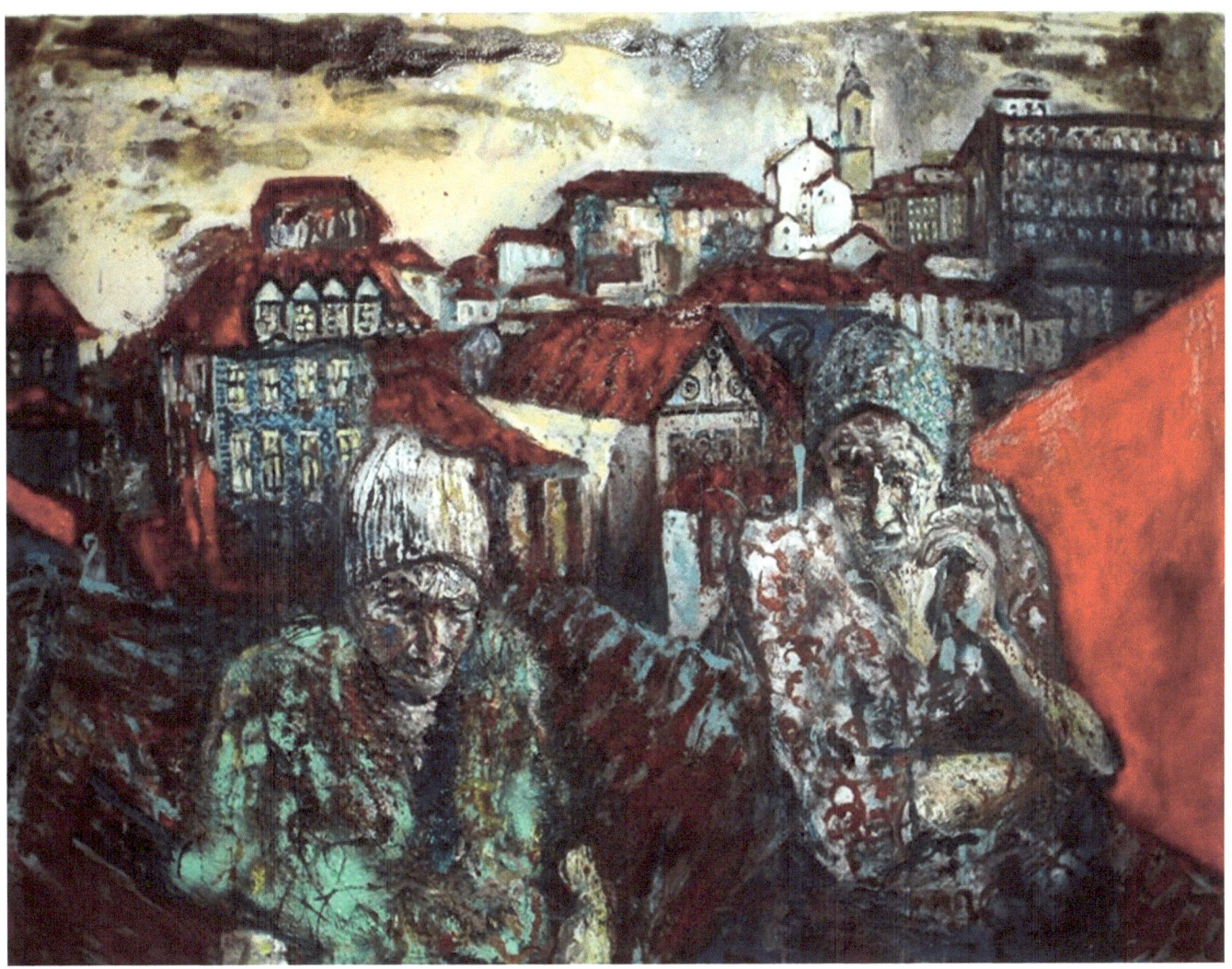

Red Roofs. Oil on canvas, 2007

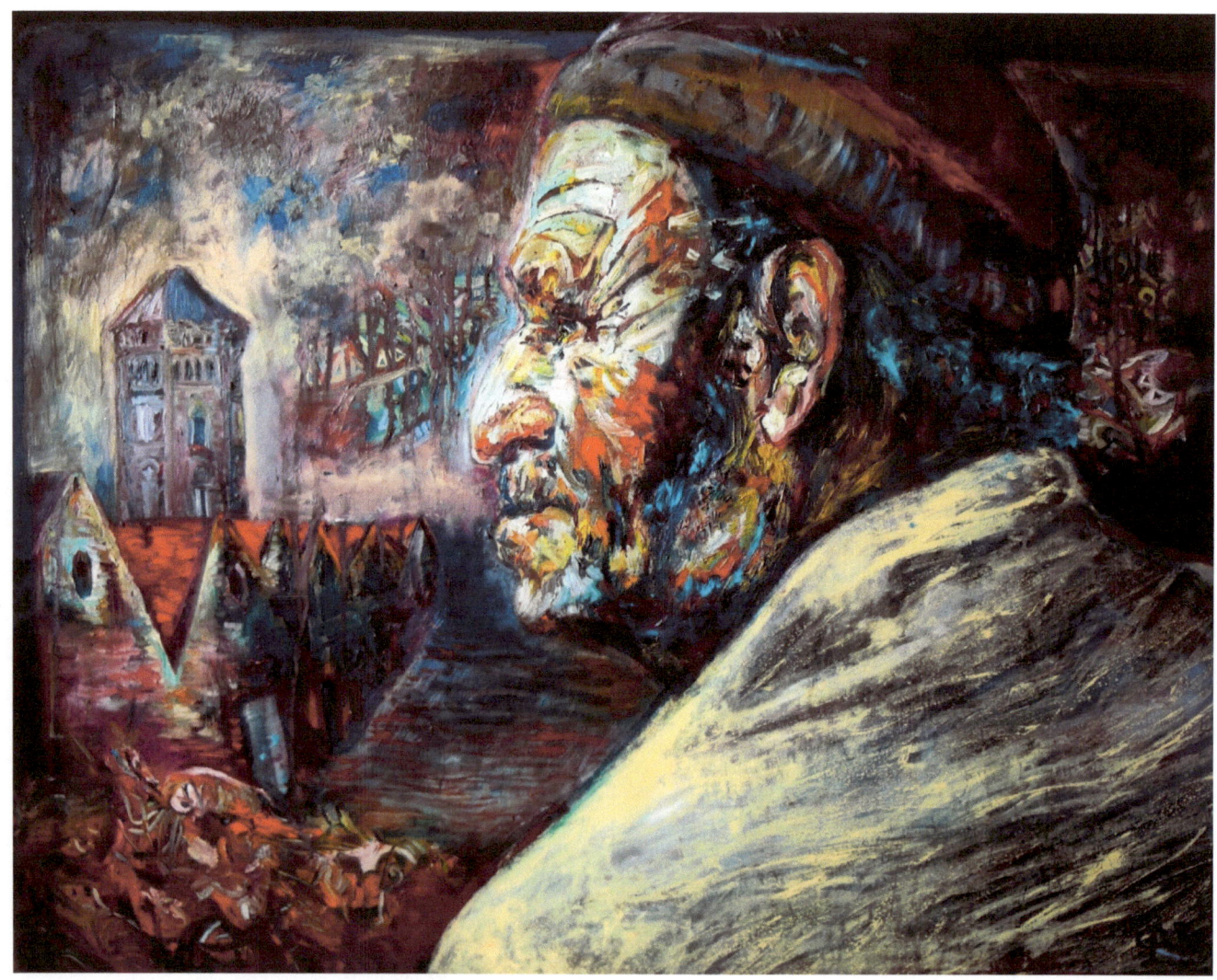

Fisherman from Sicily. Oil on canvas, 120 x 100 cm, 2007. Private collection

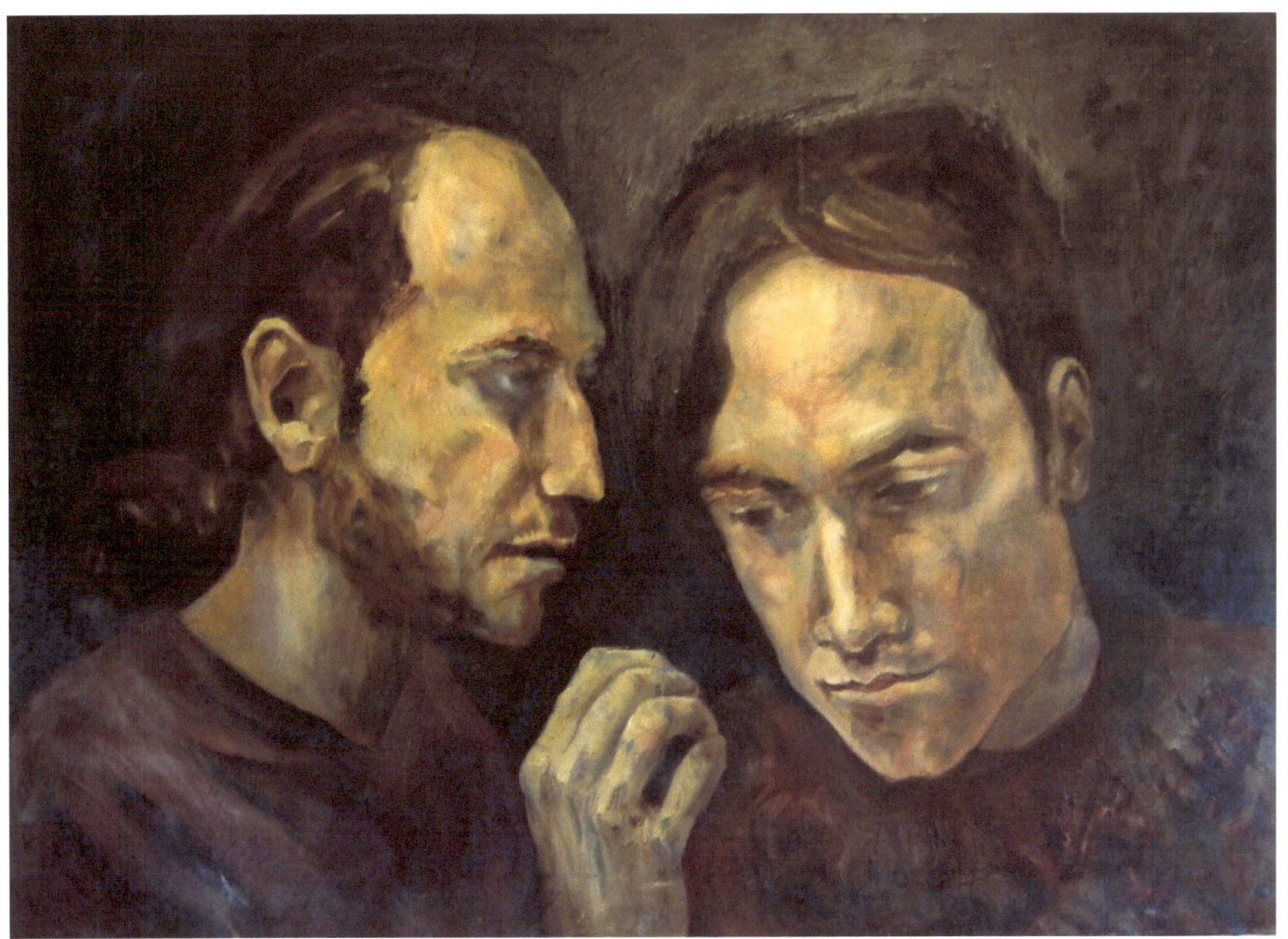

Conversation. Oil on canvas, 108 x 76 cm, 2005

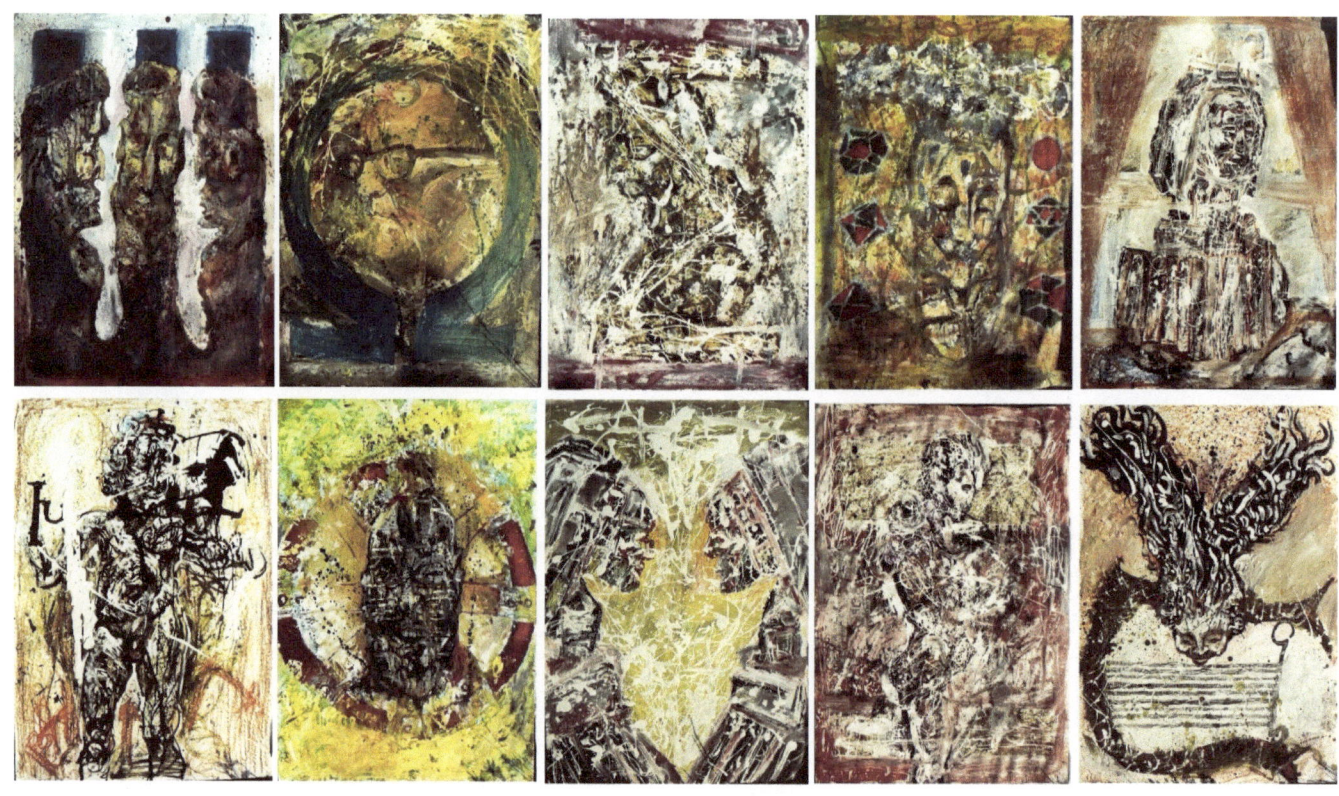

SH-O-S-T-A-K-O-V-I-CH (letters). 10 pictures: acrylic paint on paper A1 each, 2005

Murals

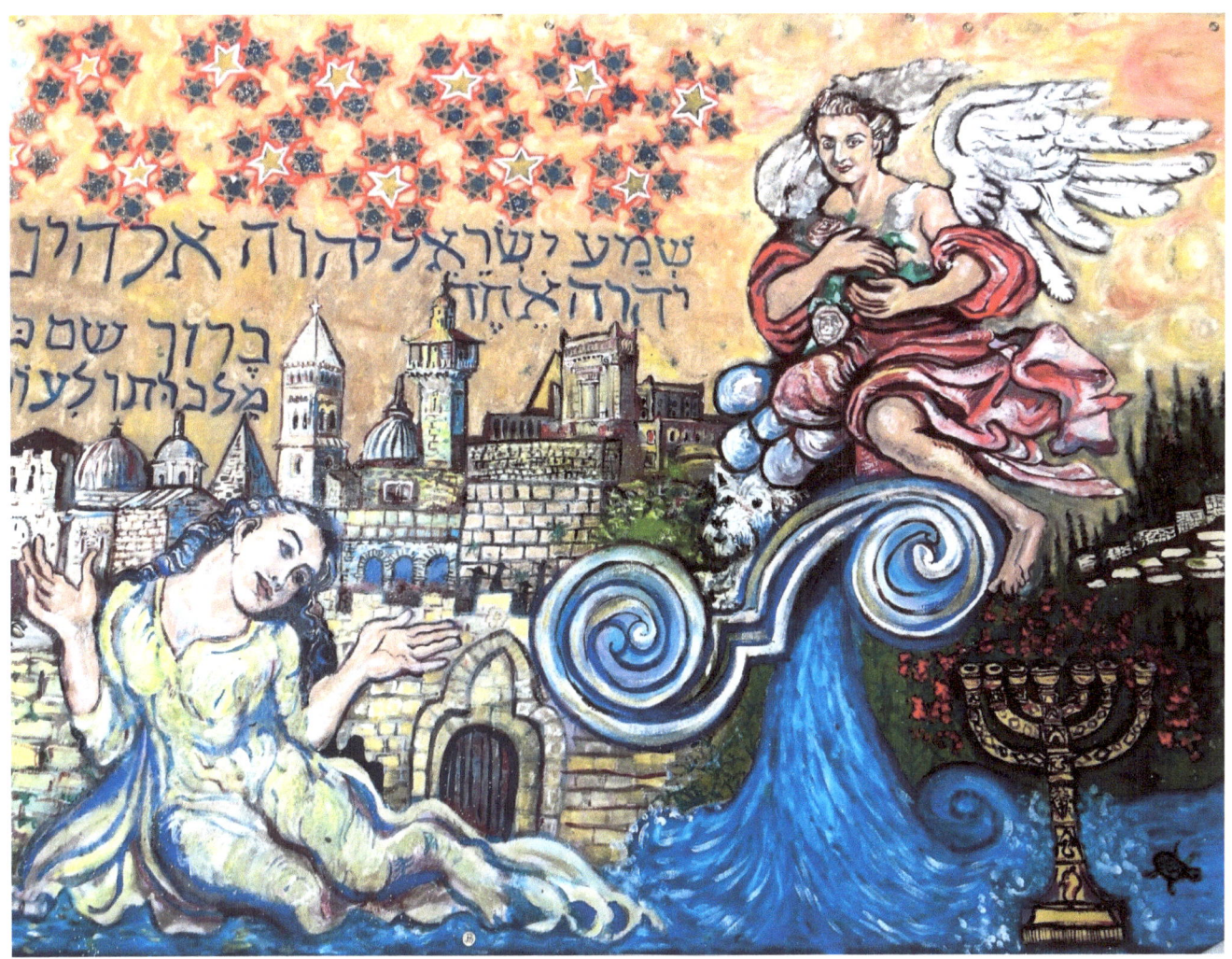

Jerusalem Mural. Acrylic, 500 x 100 cm, 2017 (detail)

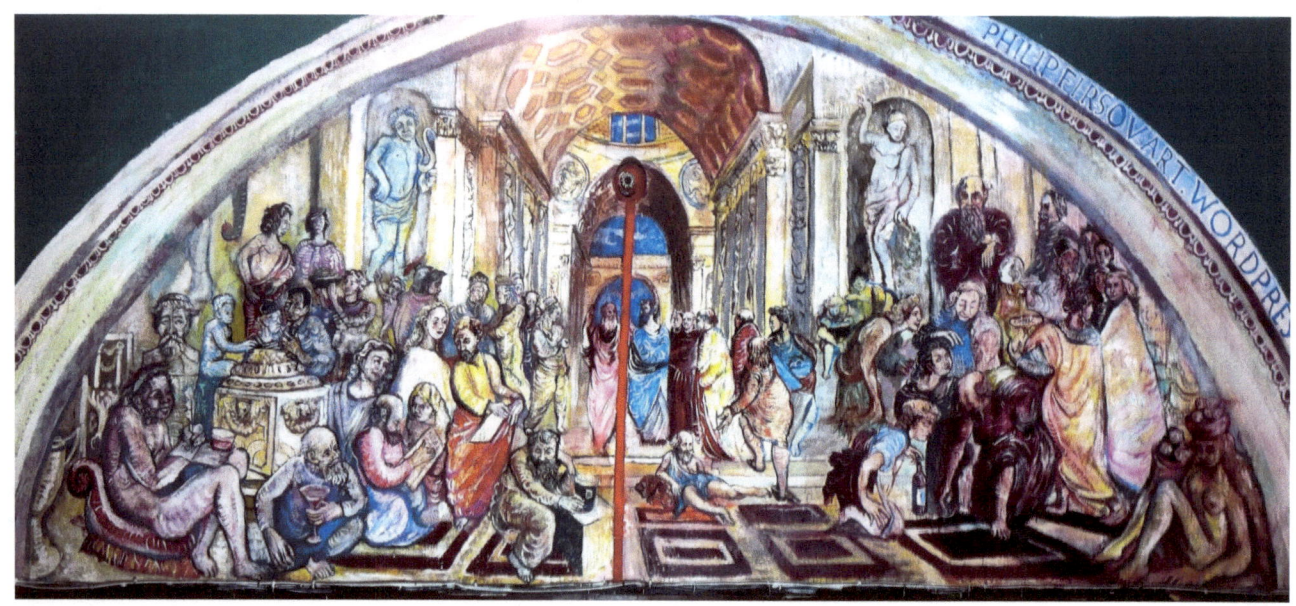

Plato's Academy. Mural, Hootananny Pub, London, 2015

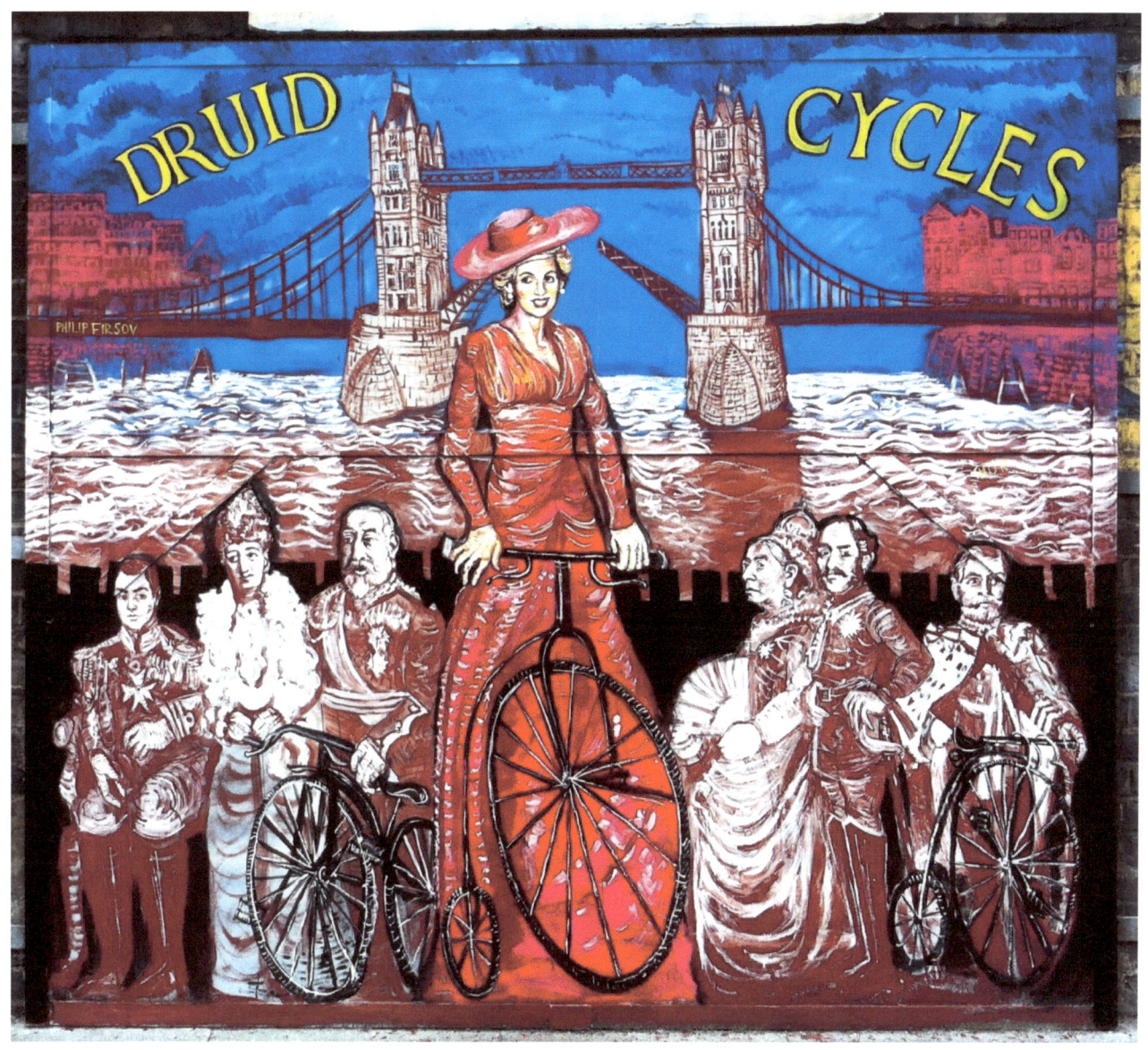

Diana Mural. Tower Bridge Road. Acrilic, 2015

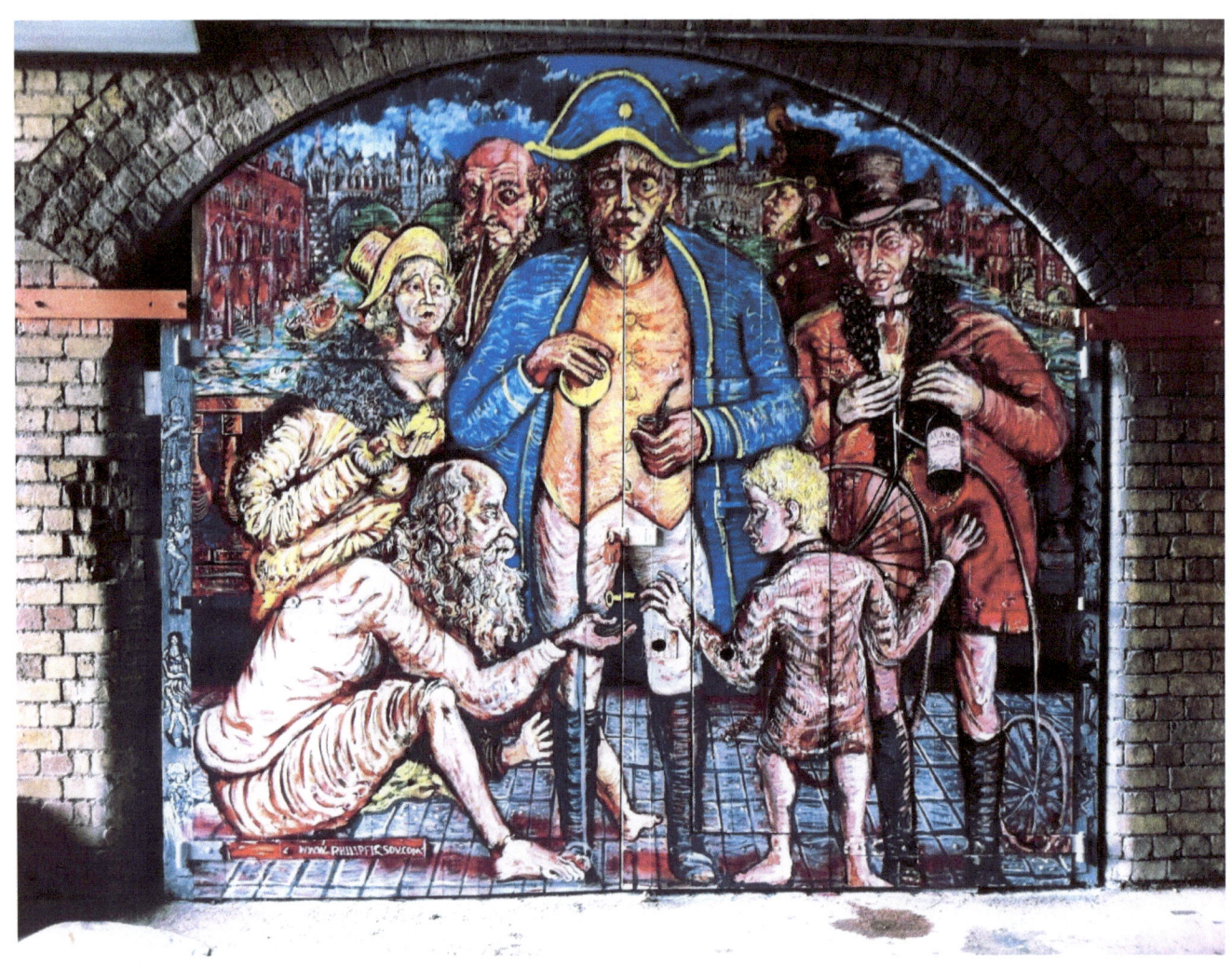

Scene from Dickens: Oliver Twist. Acrilic, 2014

Watercolours

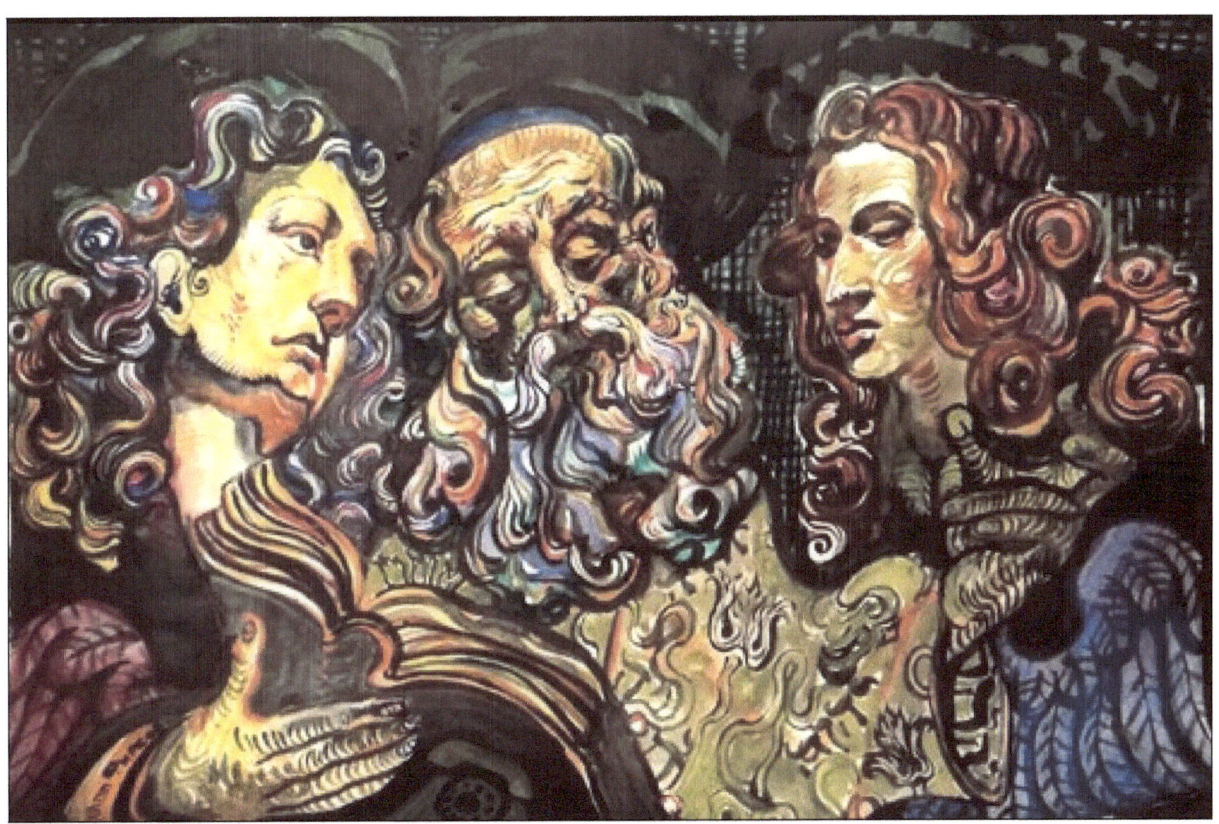

Munich Chorus. Watercolour, A1 2017. Private collection

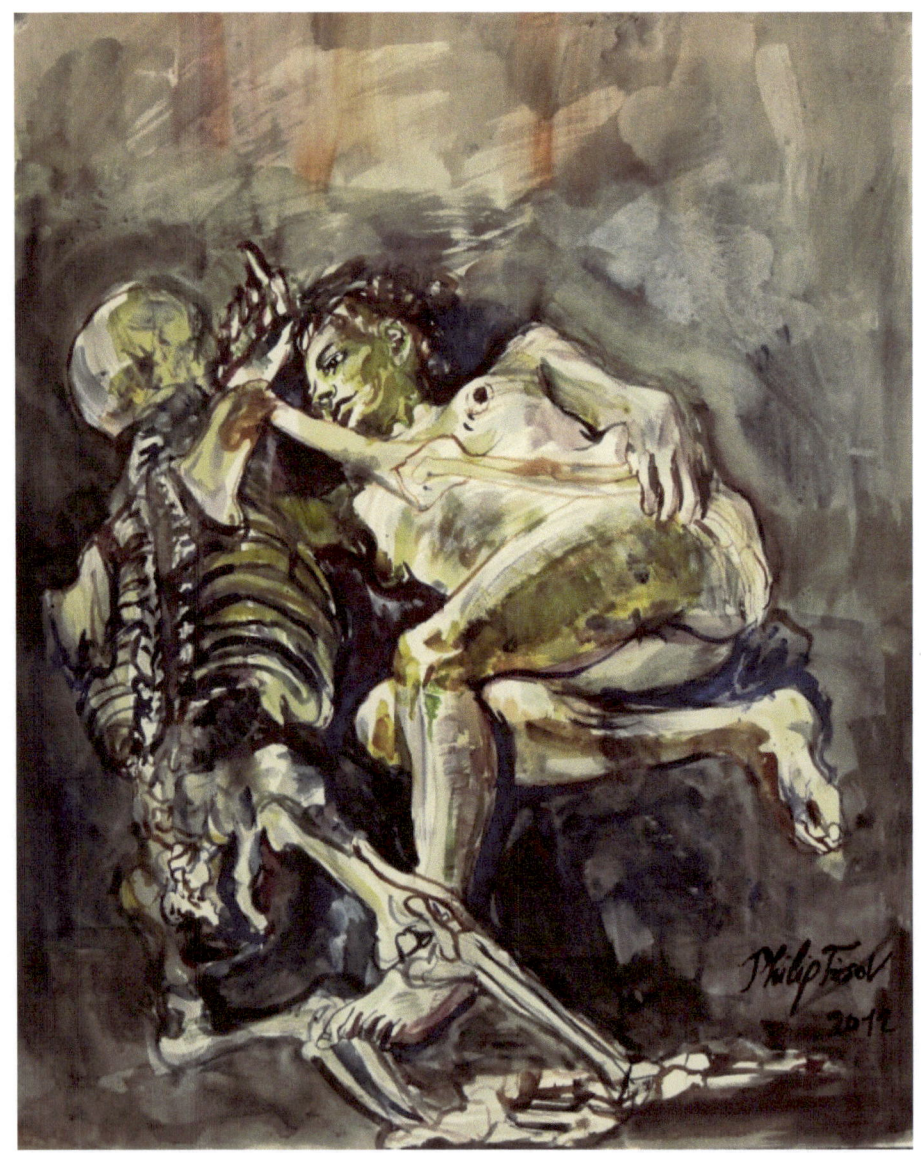

Skeleton Dance Watercolour, 2012

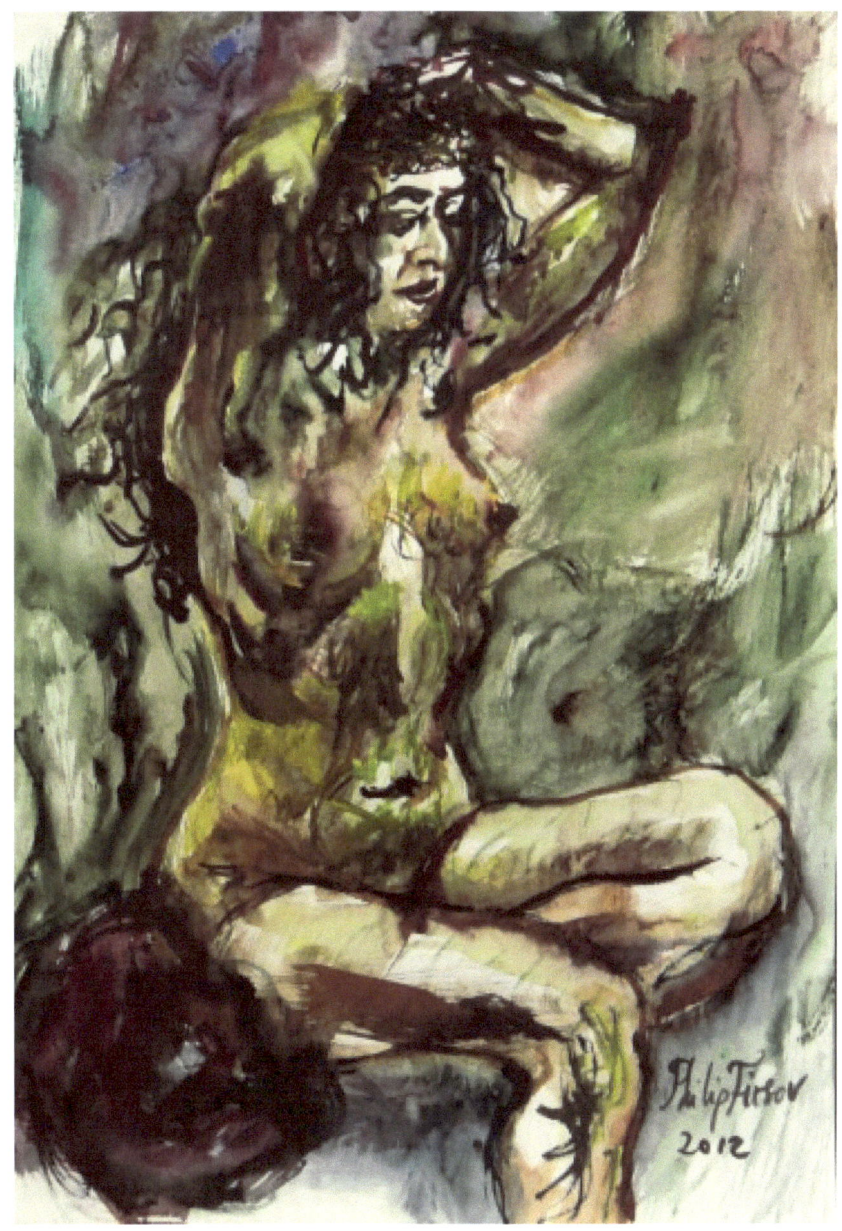

Nude. Watercolour, 2013

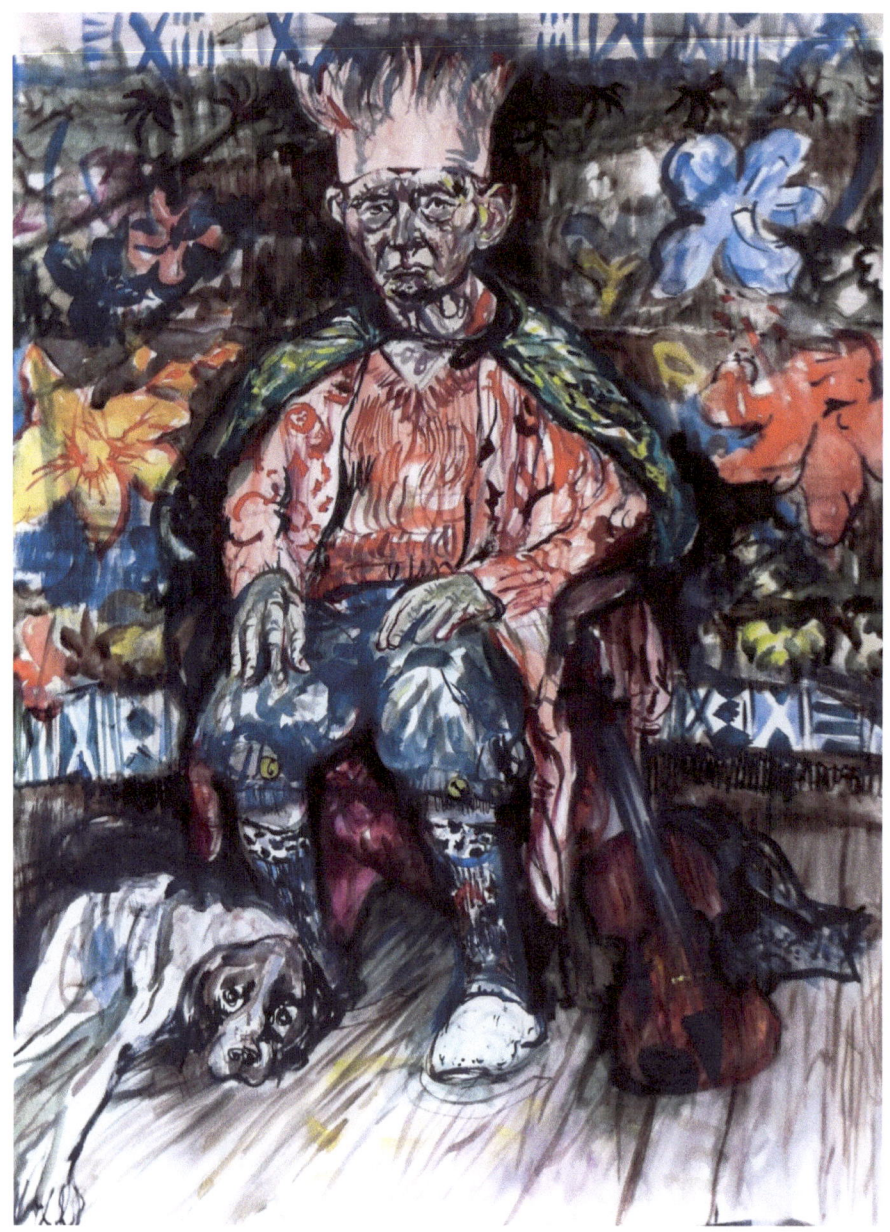

Prospero. Watercolour, 2013

Drawings

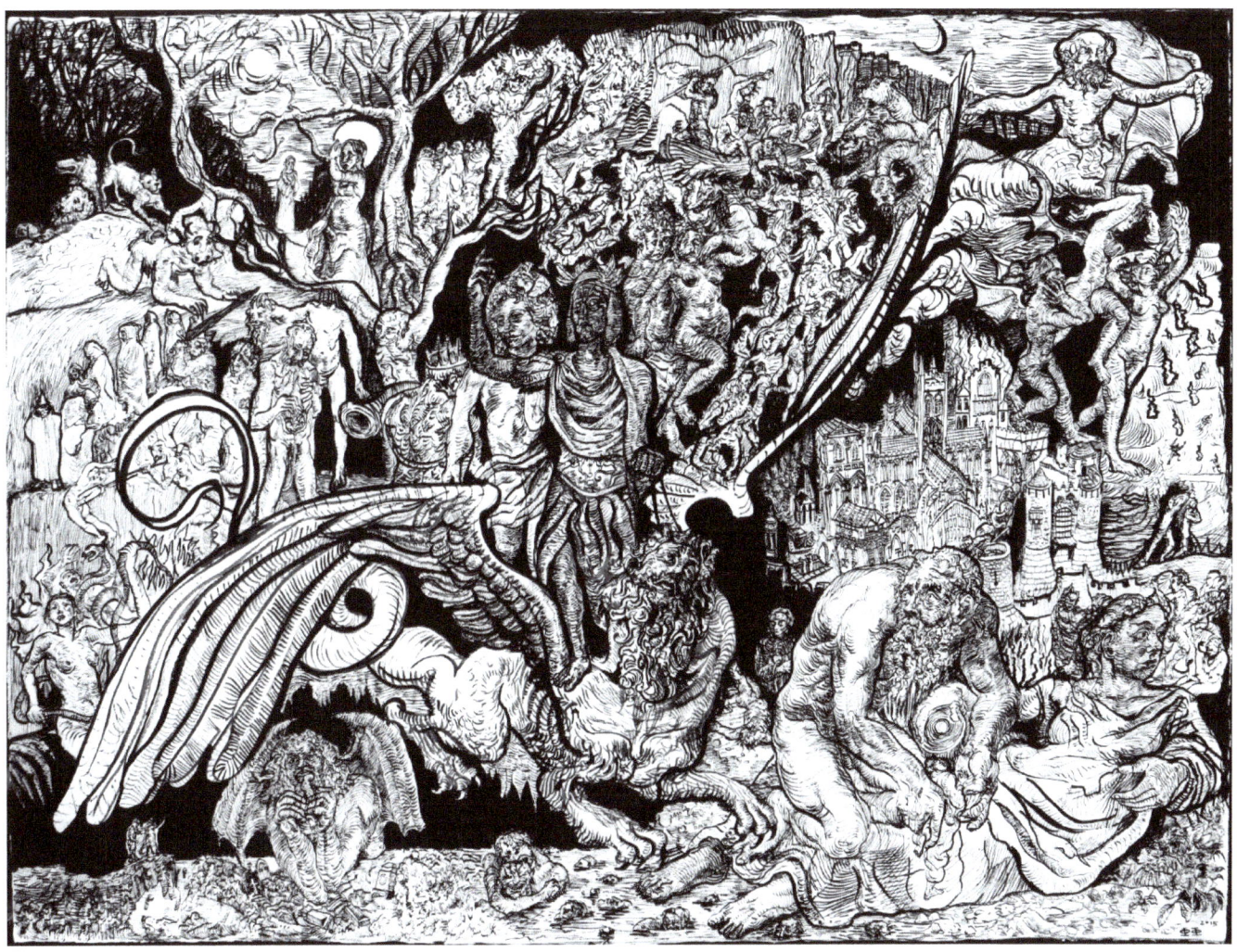

Inferno. Drawing: Indian ink, paper, A1, 2015. Private collection

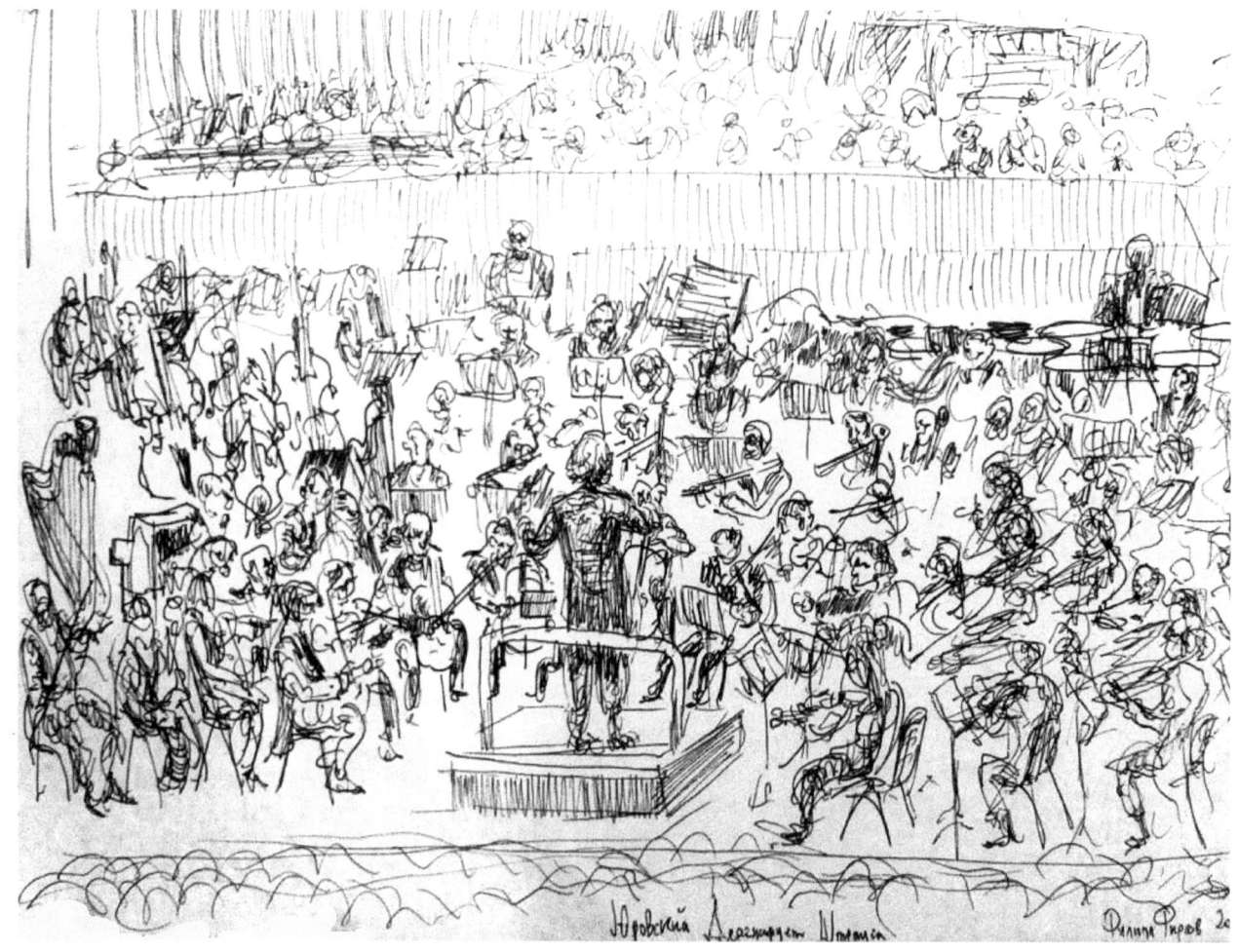

Vladimir Yurovsky conducts Strauss. Sketch: pen on paper, 2013. Private collection

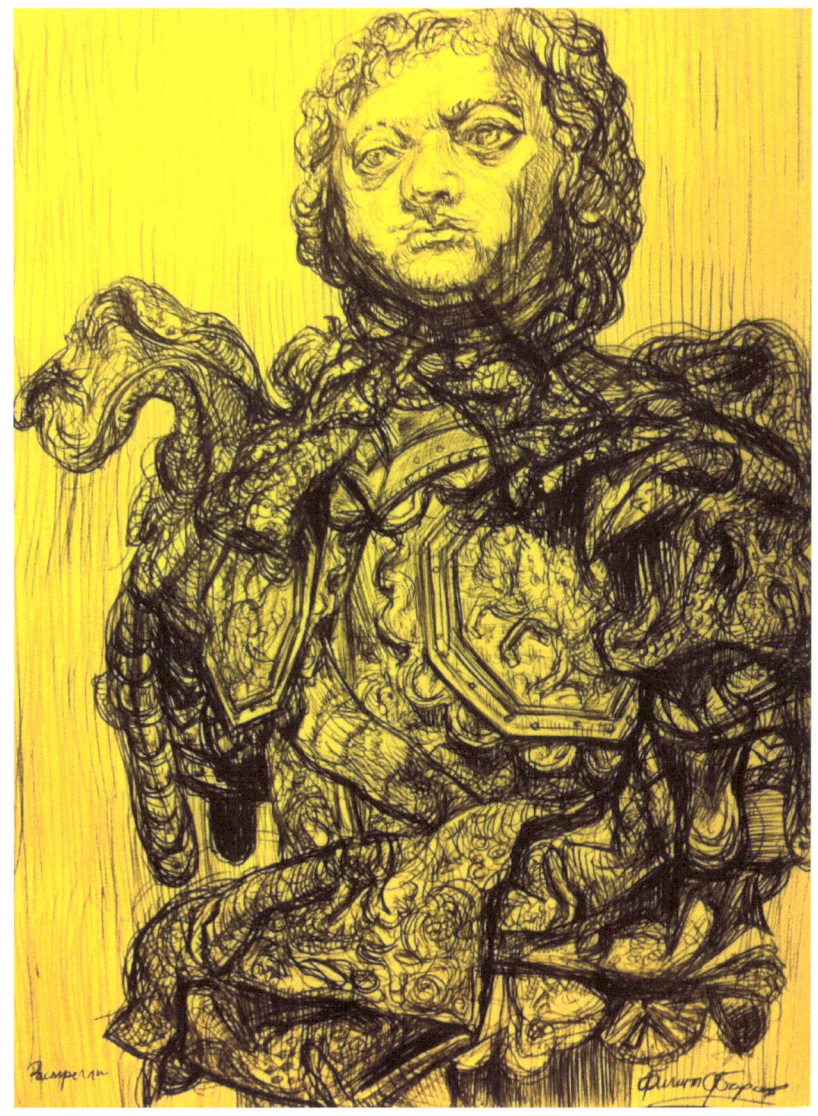

Peter the Great by Carlo Rastrelli. Pen, yellow paper. 2013

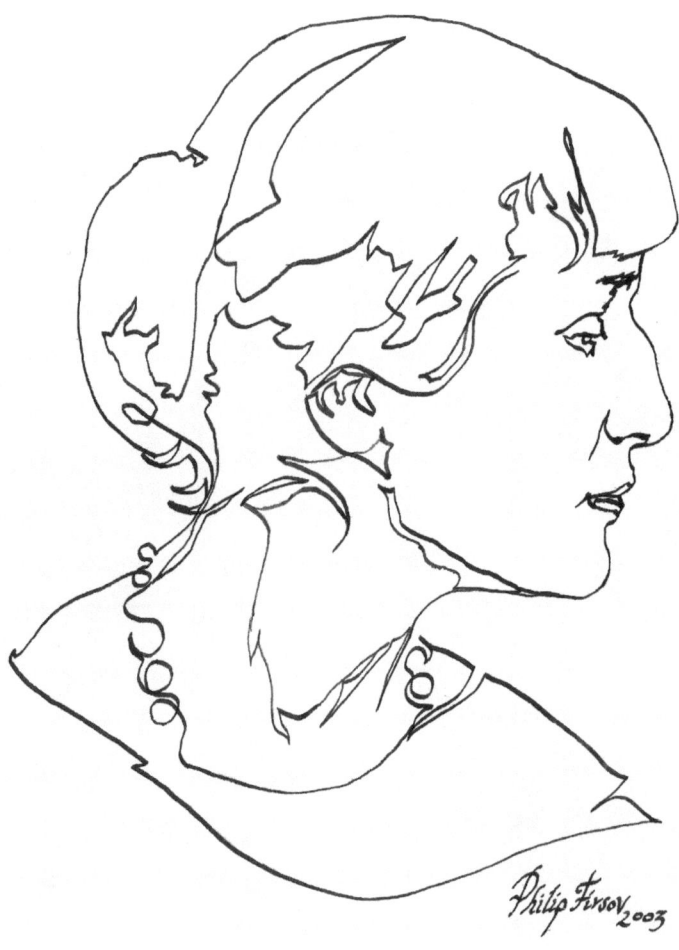

Anna Akhmatova. Line drawing: Indian ink on paper, 2003

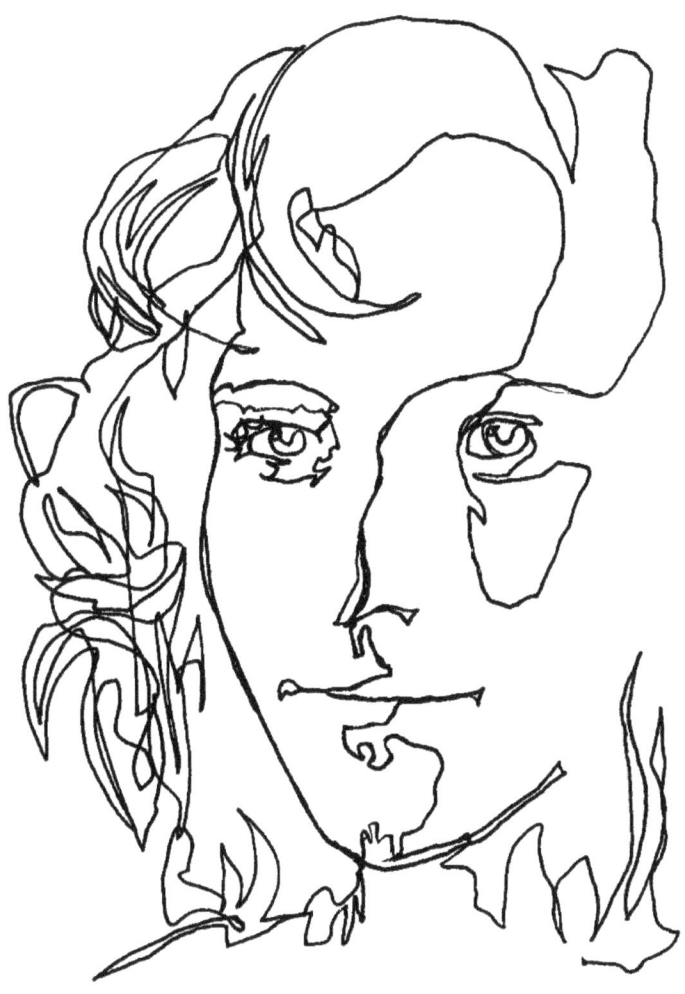

Mother (Elena Firsova). Line drawings: Indian ink on paper, 2000

Etchings

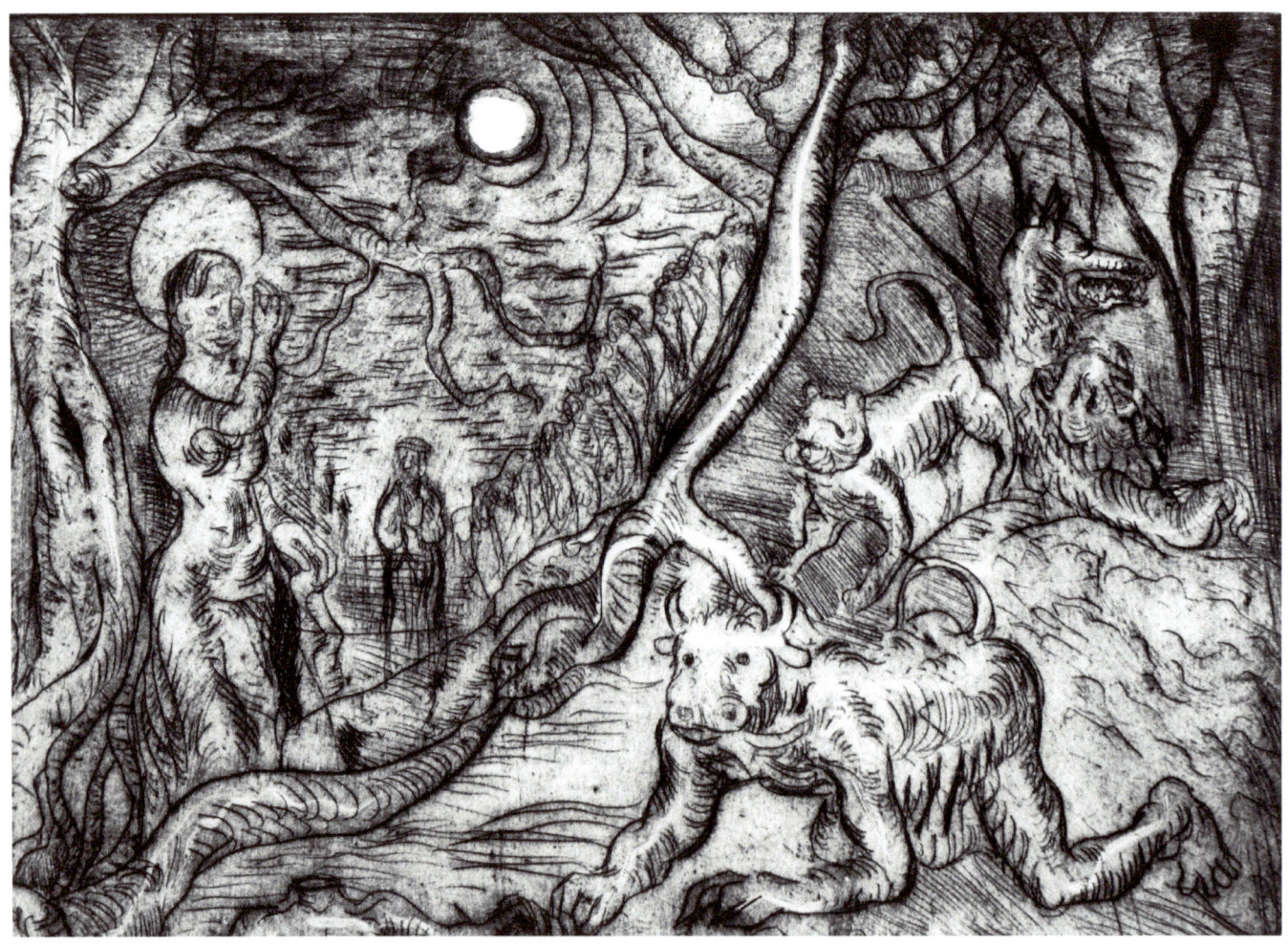

Inferno. Engraving, A1, 2016. Detail: Beatrice, Virgil & Three Beasts

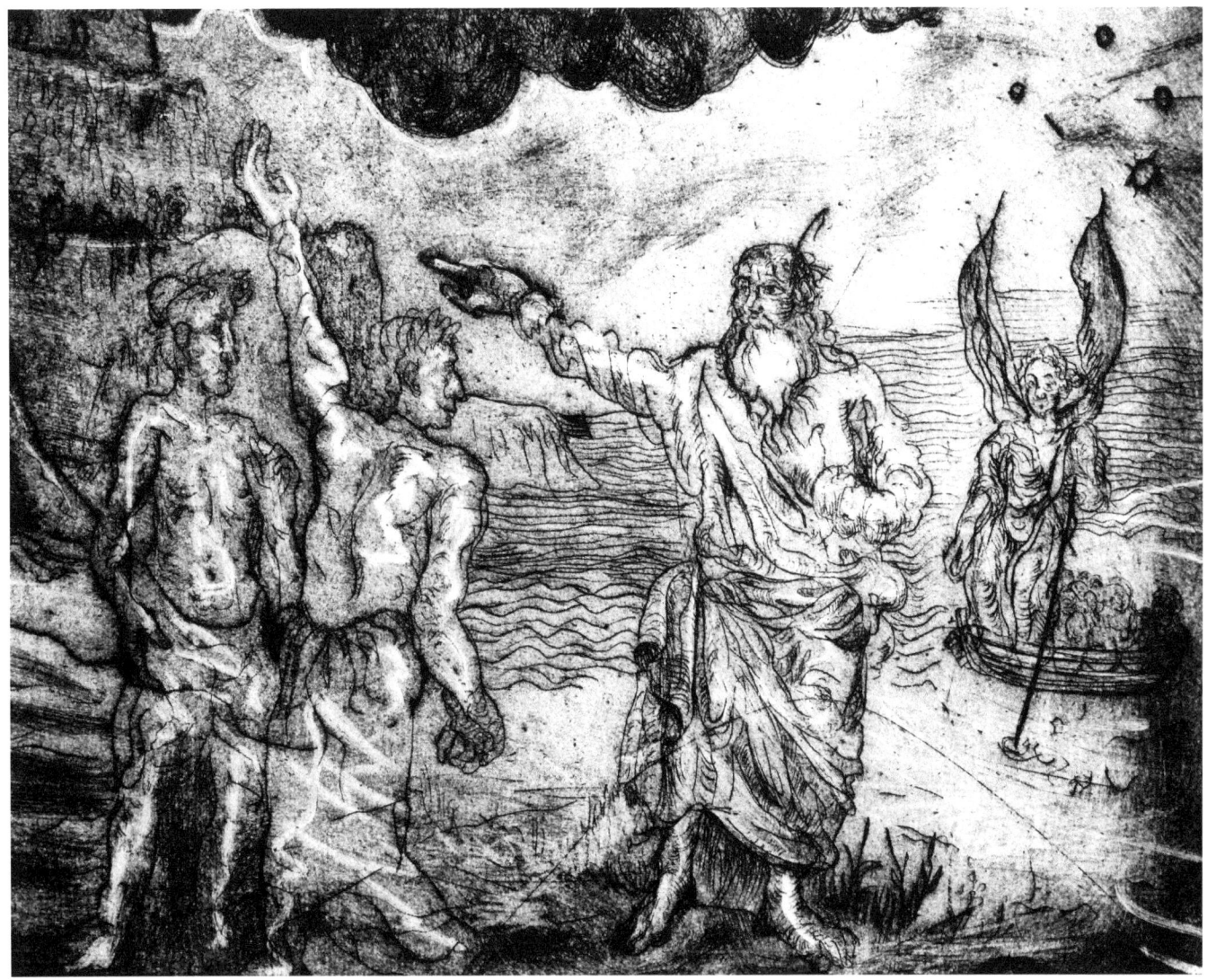

Purgatorio. Engraving, A1, 2016. Detail: Virgil, Dante and Cato of Utica

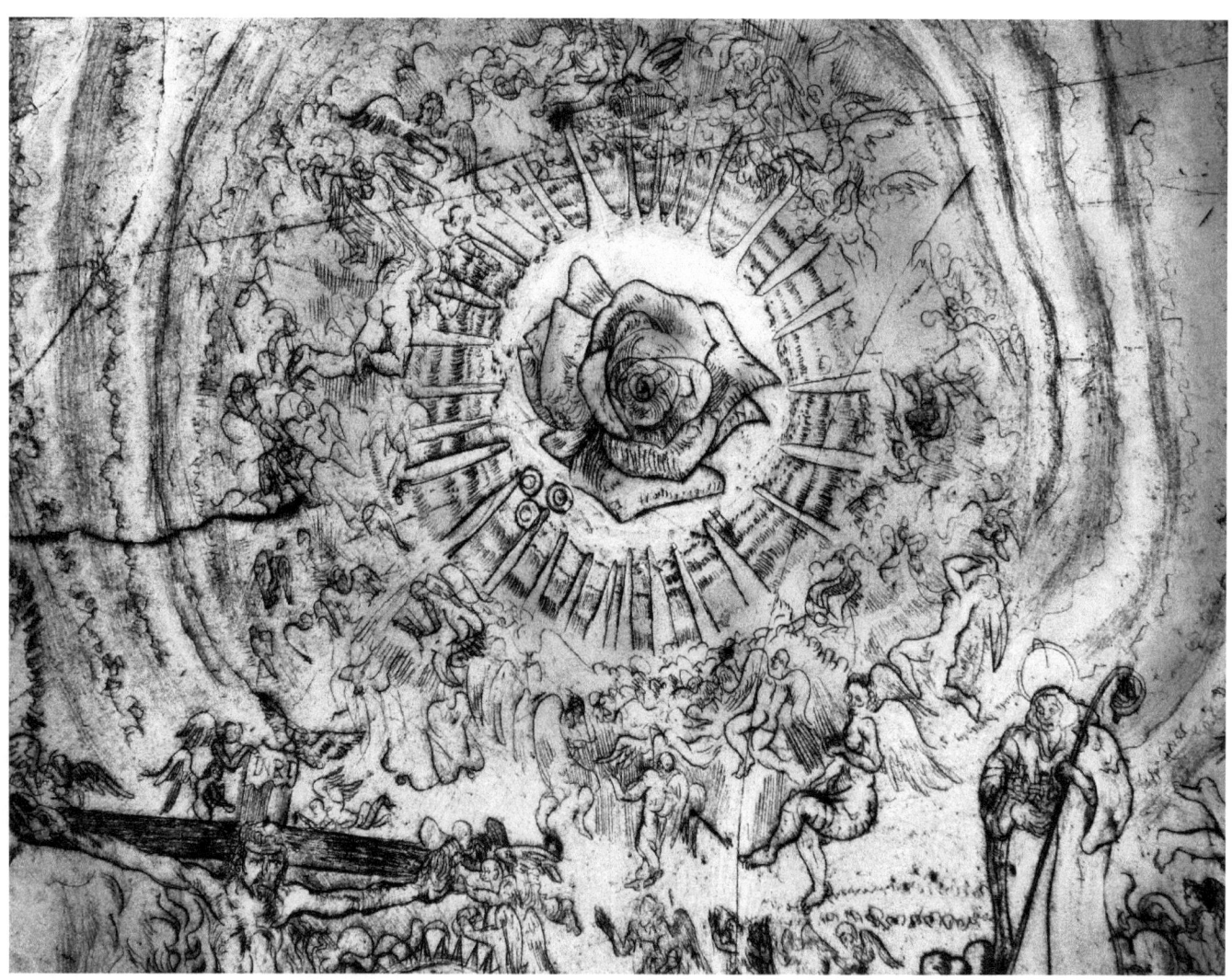

Paradiso. Engraving, A1, 2016. Detail: Empyrean or the Heavenly Rose

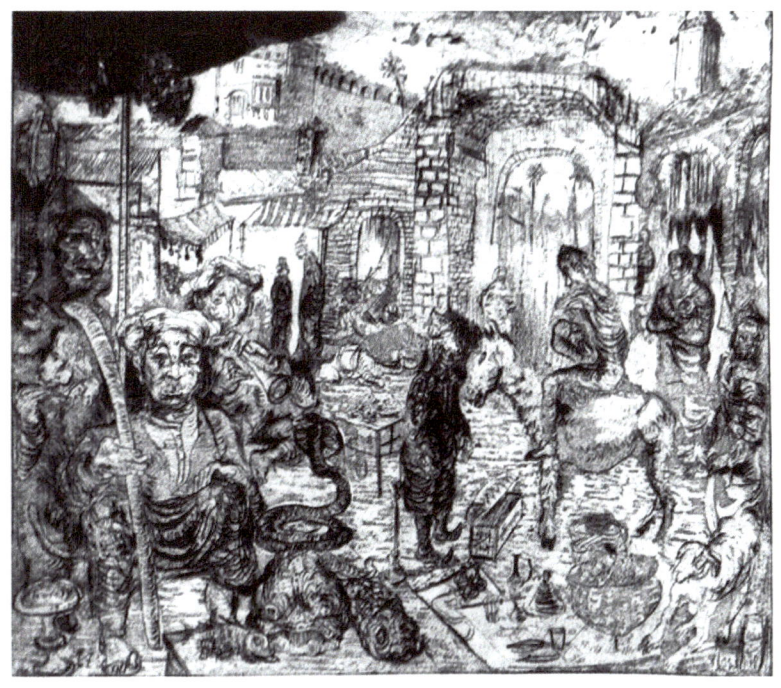

Essaouira, Morocco. Etching, 2015

Essaouira, Morocco

After a day of sketching at the bazaar in Morocco, I composed a holistic narrative into the etching, the space of the traders can be entered from many directions and the myriad of choices of curiosity can arrest the eye on the laid out carpets, where snake charmers and monkfish display striking actuality. The city in the background winds into camel trails beneath sandstone minarets and the sun bakes the turbans and umbrellas of timeless trader stereotypes.

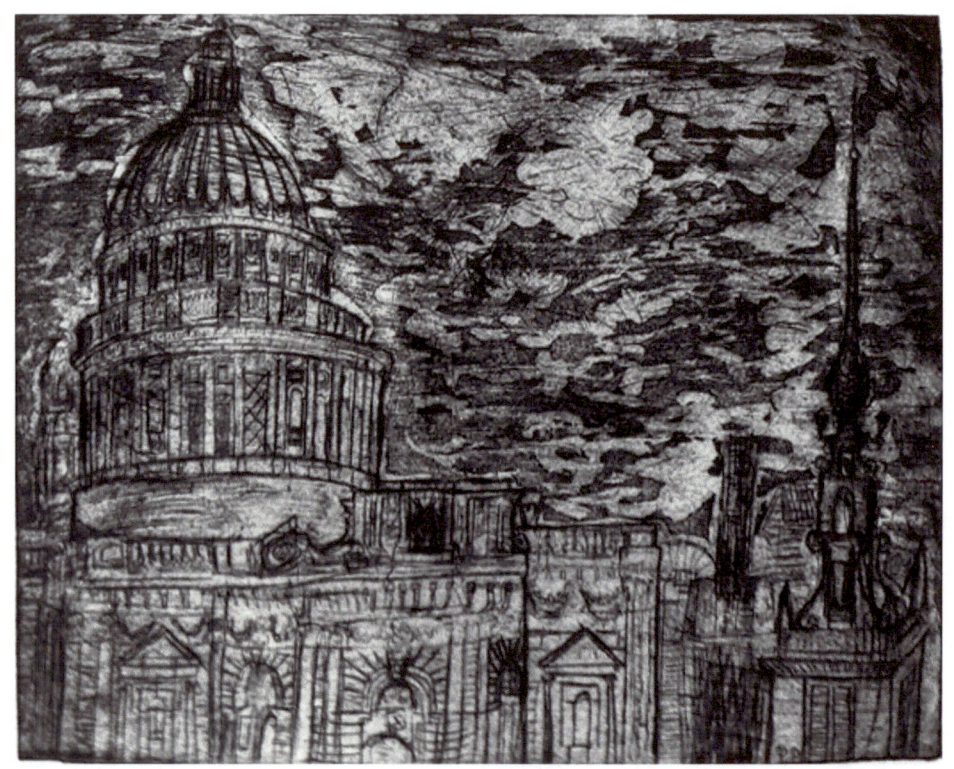

St Paul's. Etching, 2014

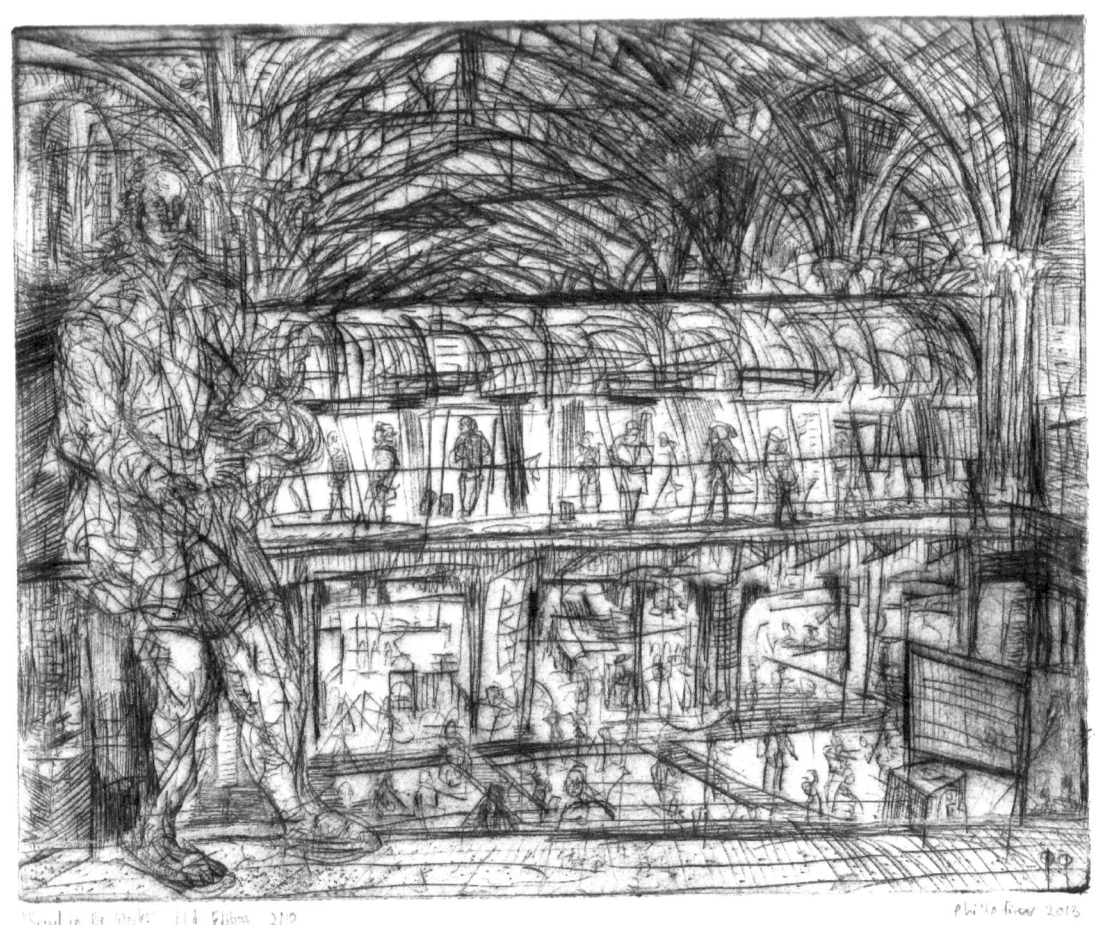

Isambard Kingdom Brunel in the Works. Etching, 2013

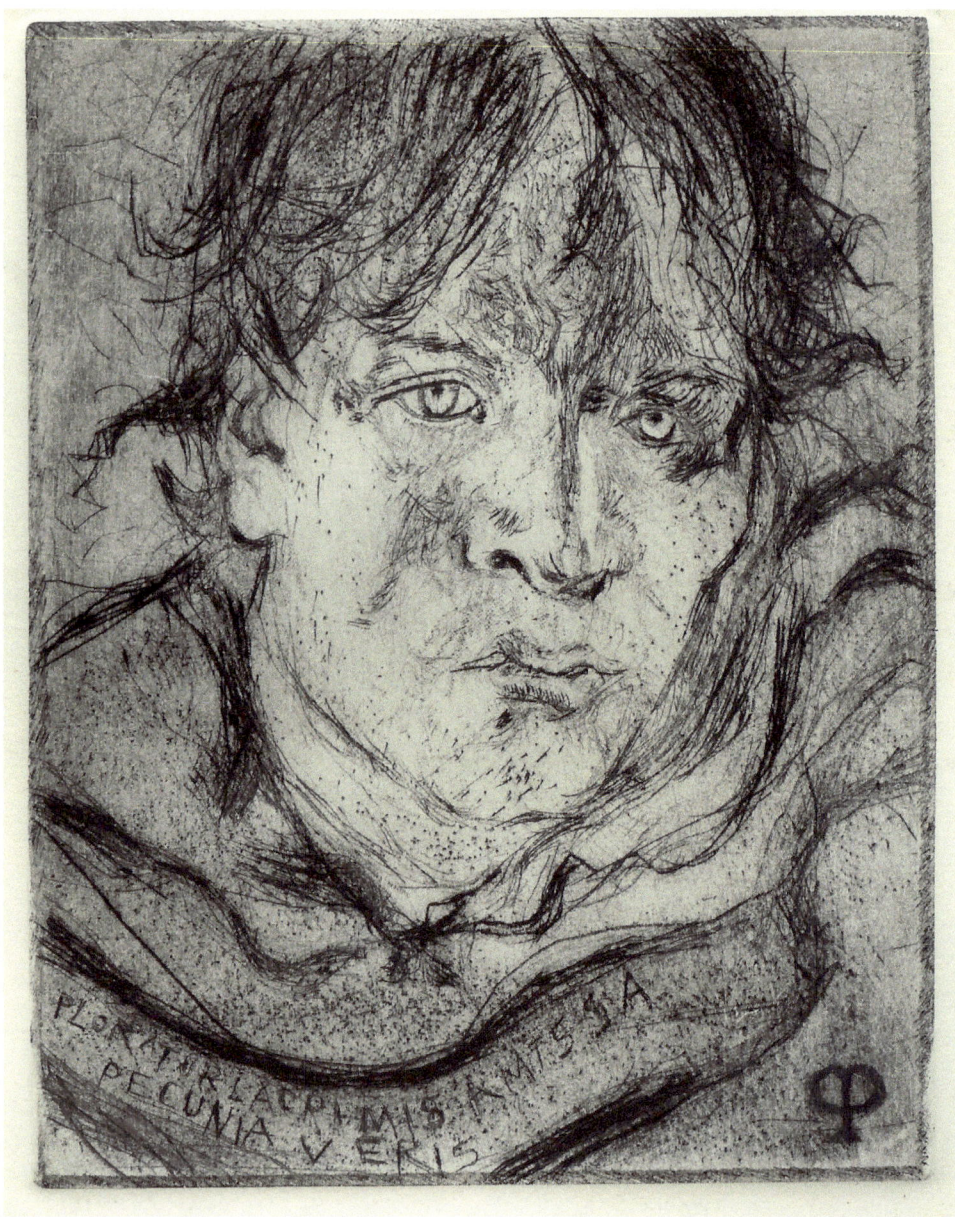

Self Portrait. Etching, 2009

Sculptures

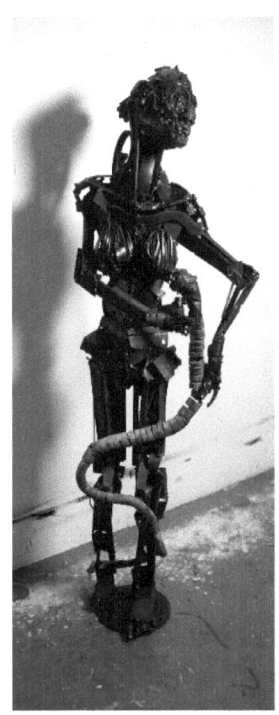 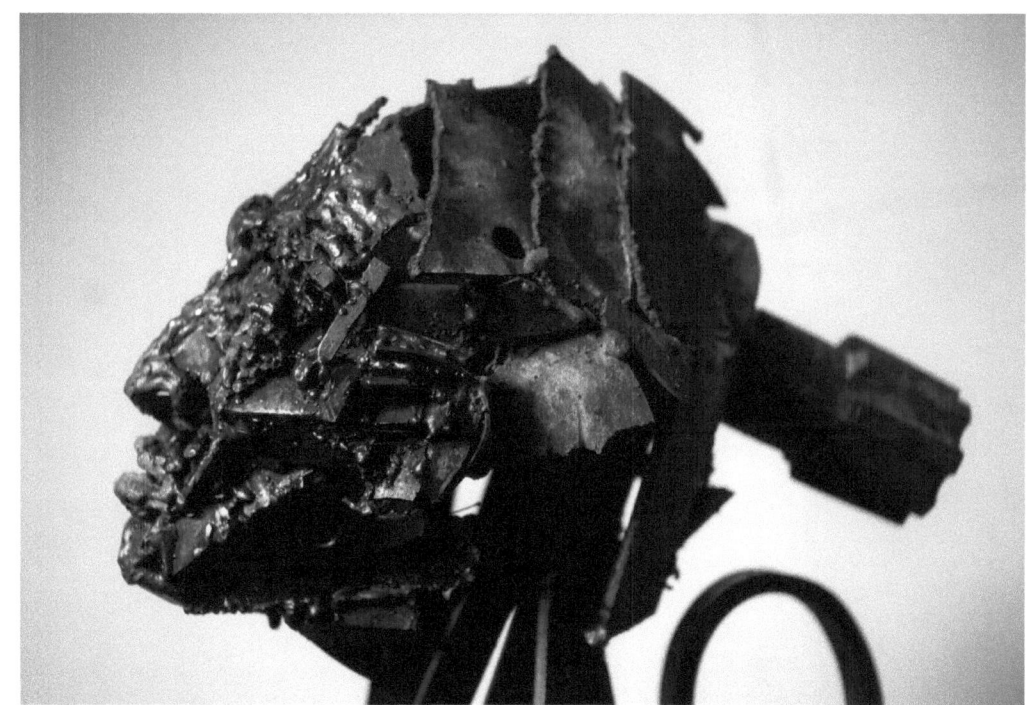

Cleopatra. Steel welding, 2007. Private collection.

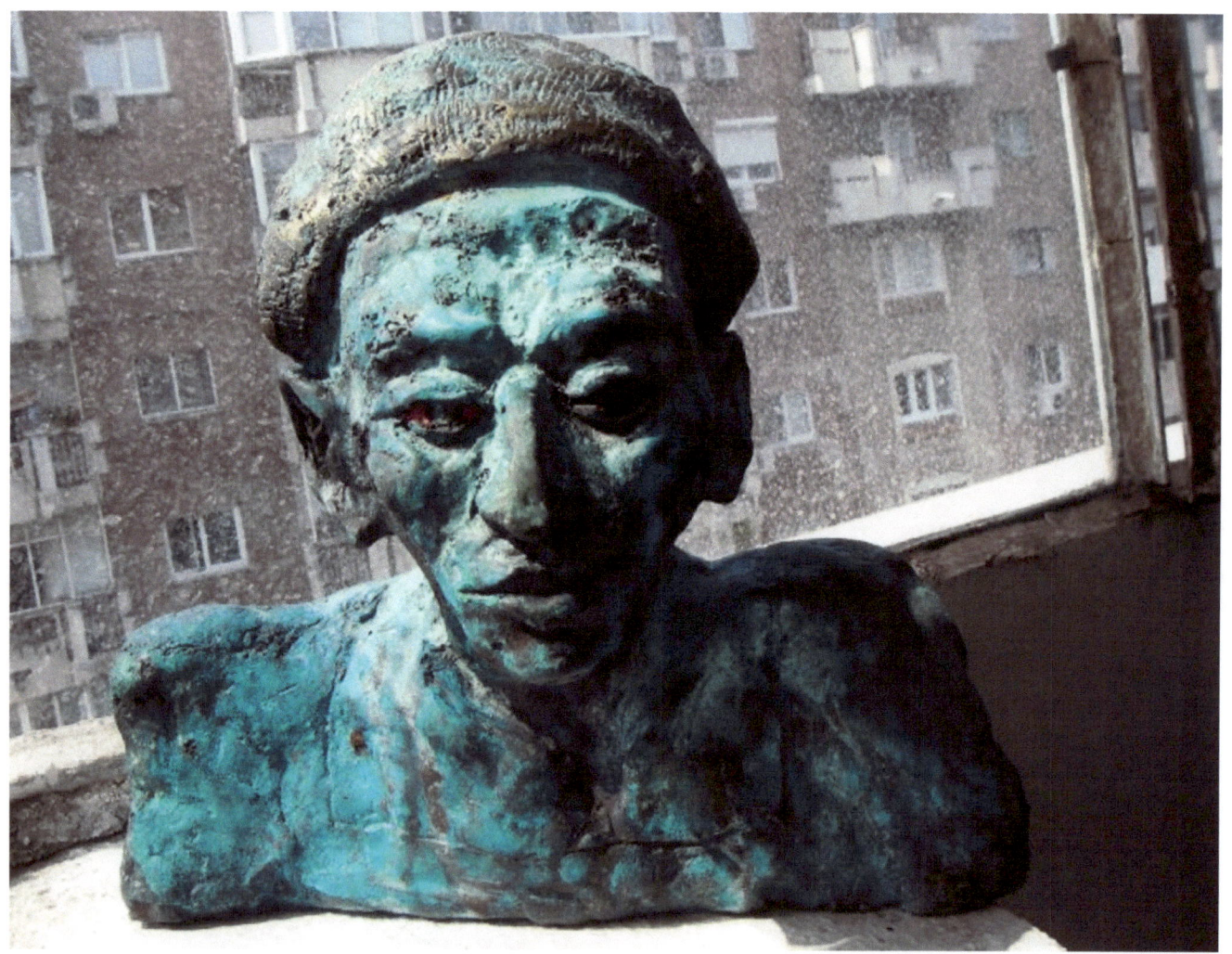

Dracula. Bronze with blue patina, 2008

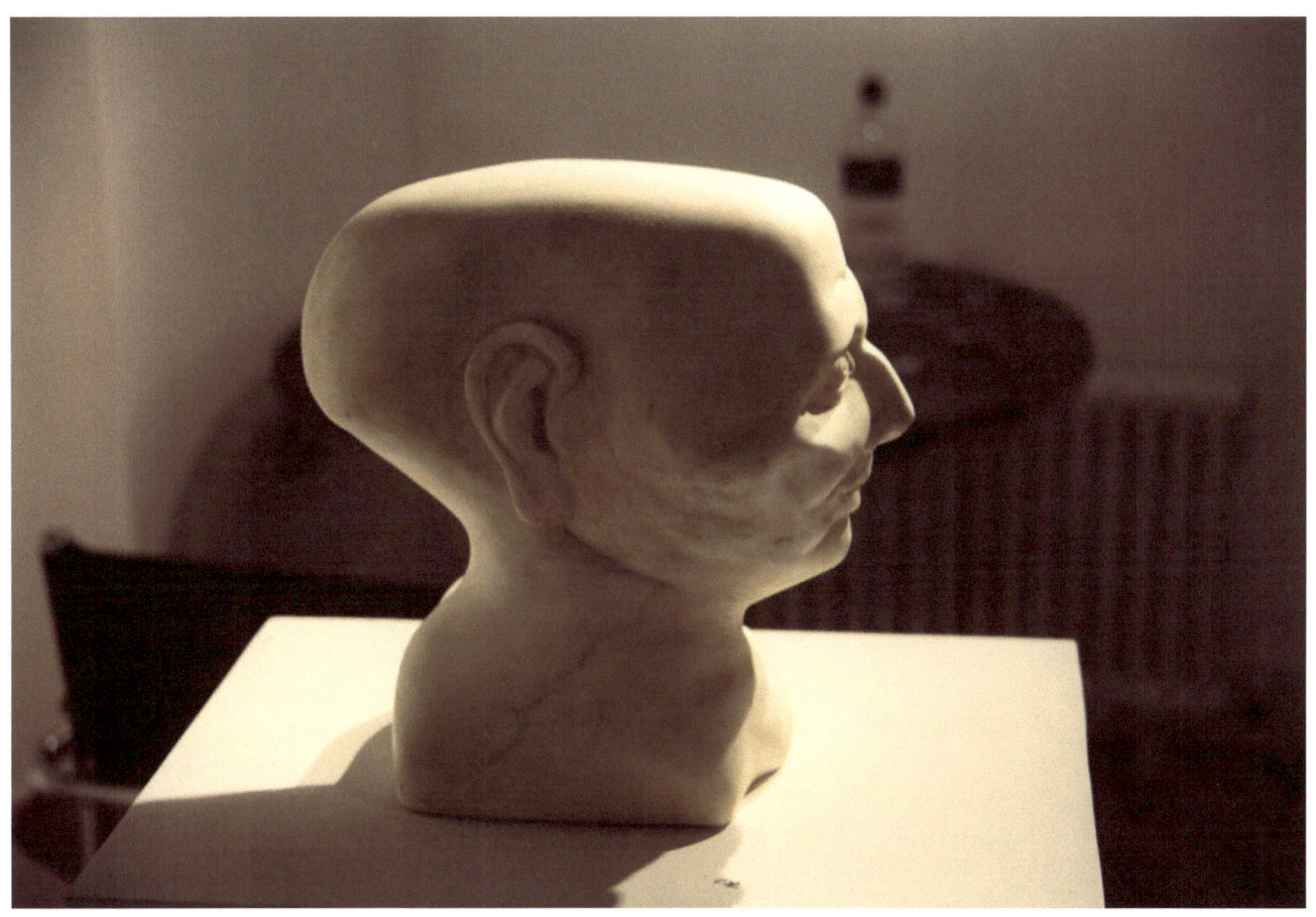

Alien Head. Carrara Marble, 2009

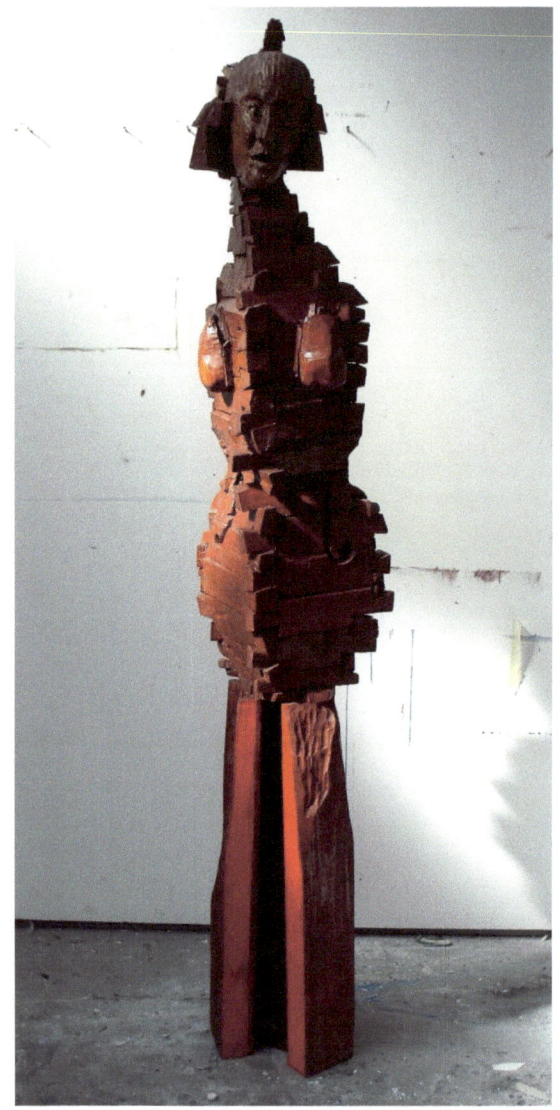 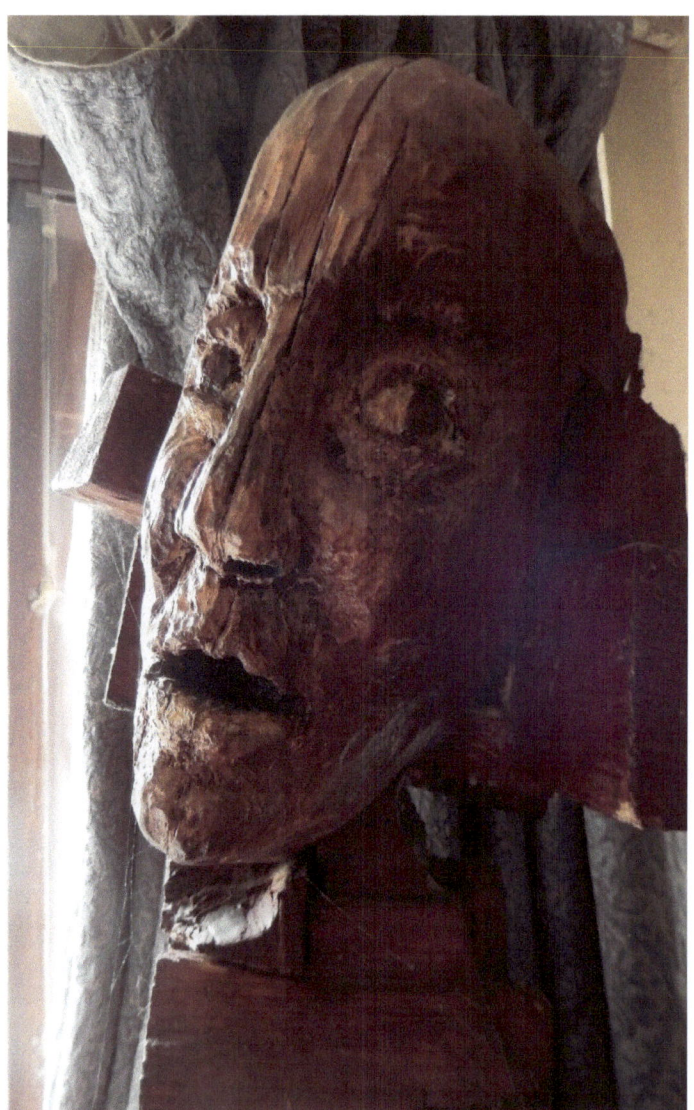

Woman Cello. Wood, 2006

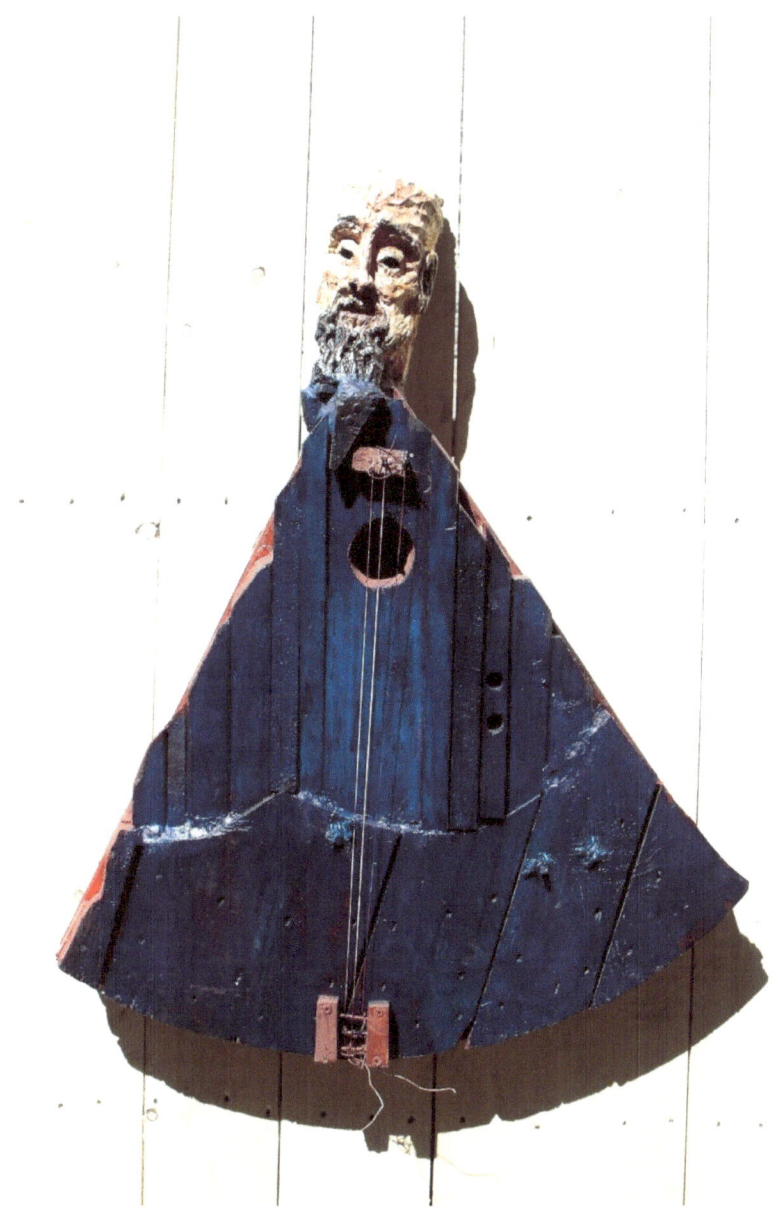

Balalaika Man. Wood, wire, 2006

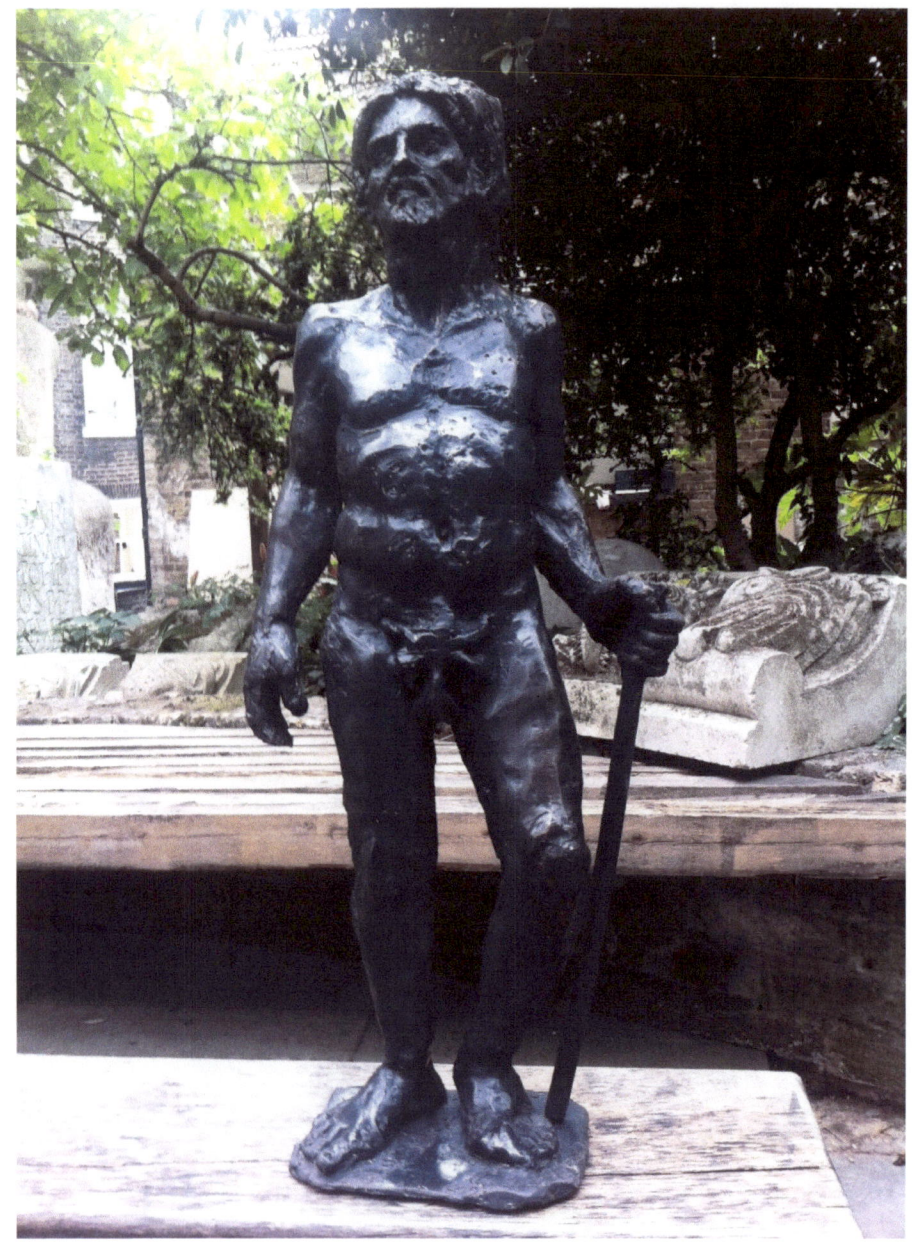

The Emperor. Bronze, 2016

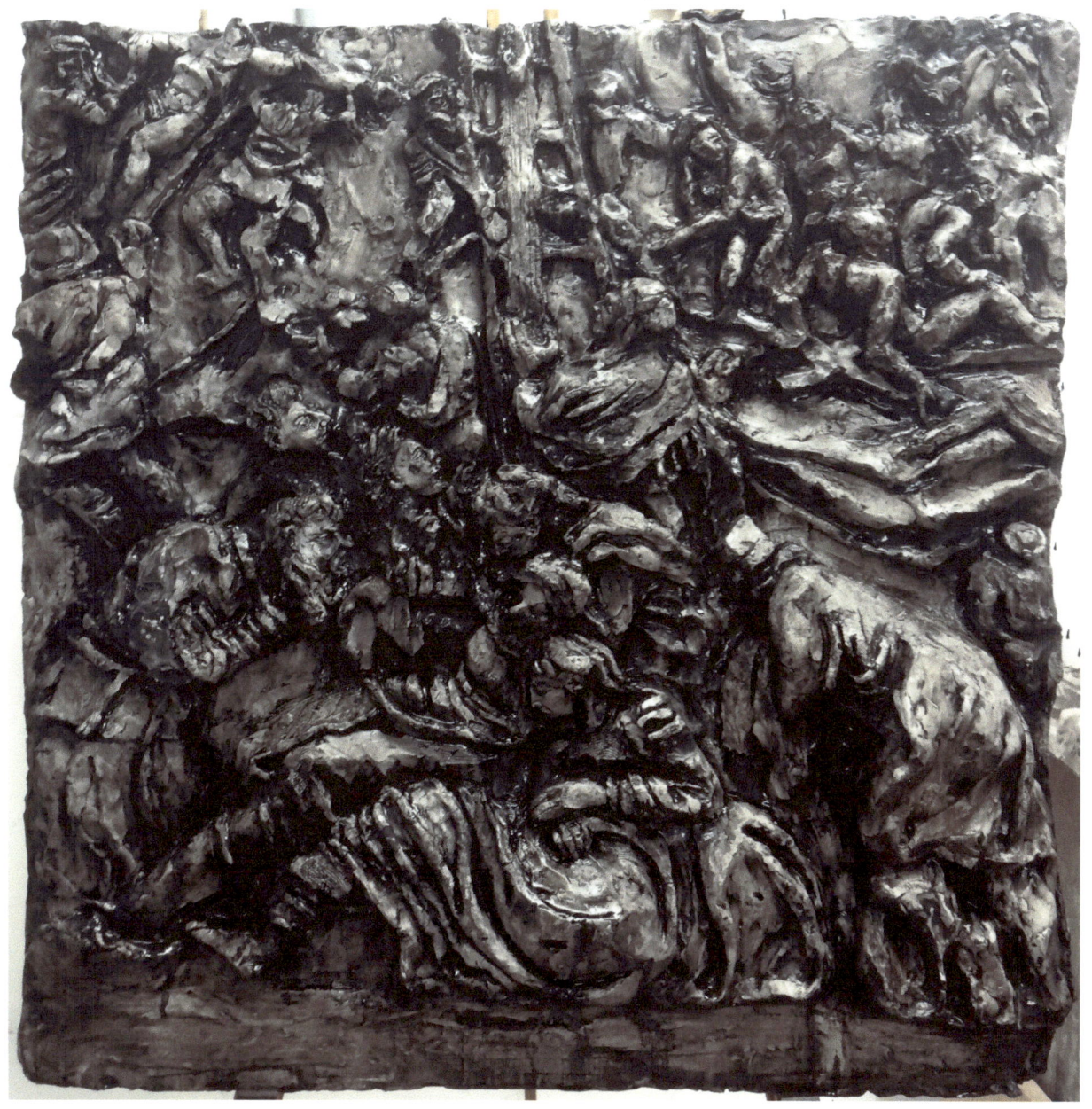

The Bewailing: *STABAT MATER DOLOROSA*. After Tintoretto relief. Cement, 2016

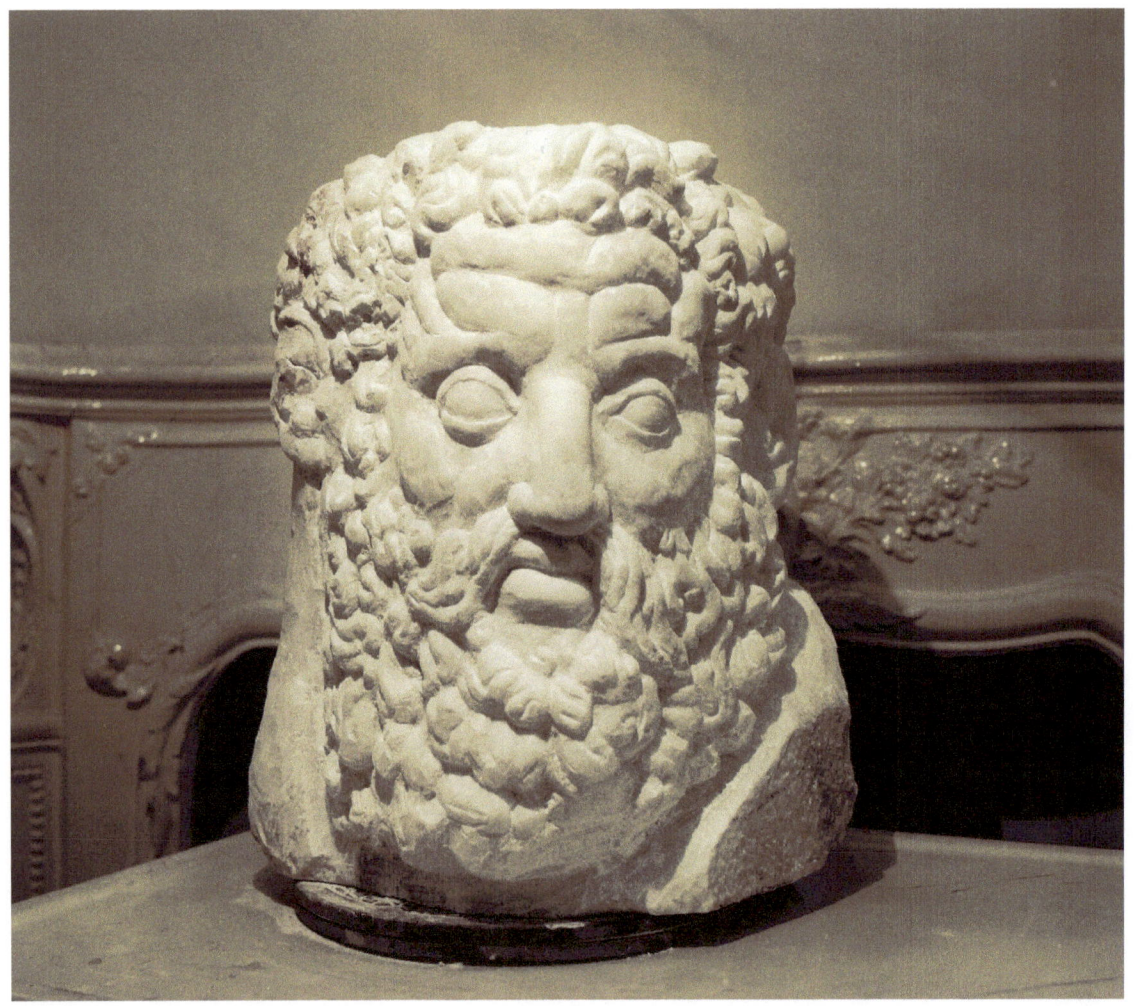

Hercules Head. Alabaster, 50 x 40 x 40 cm, 2017

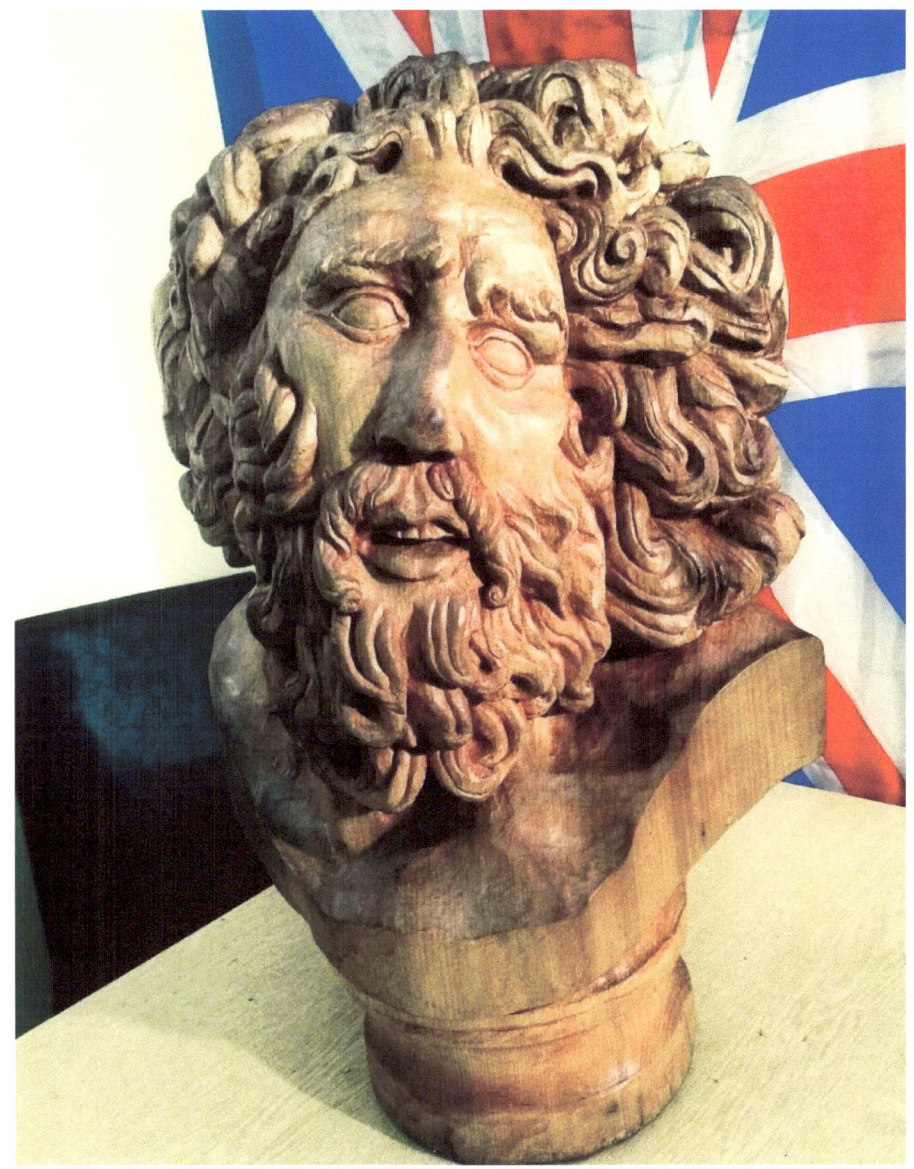

Laocoon Bust. Pine, 80 x 70 x 50 cm, 2017

www.ingramcontent.com/pod-product-compliance
Lightning Source LLC
Chambersburg PA
CBHW051204220526
45473CB00003B/895